REDDITCH

FROM THE CHIP SHOP TO THE BATCHLEY

IN MEMORY OF MUM AND DAD

REDDITCH

FROM THE CHIP SHOP TO THE BATCHLEY

Memories of a young boy growing up through the 1950s and 1960s

Tony Aston

BREWIN BOOKS

BREWIN BOOKS
19 Enfield Ind. Estate,
Redditch,
Worcestershire,
B97 6BY
www.brewinbooks.com

First published by Brewin Books 2022

Bottom front cover image by kind courtesy of RLHS / Geoff Holmes Collection – www.redditchhistorysociety.org.uk.

A CIP catalogue record for this book is available from the British Library.

ISBN: 978-1-85858-744-8

Printed and bound in Great Britain by Dig Print.

Contents

Acknowledgements 6

Foreword 7

1. The Early Days – 1953 to 1958 9

2. Granny and Grandad – Jack and Nellie Thornton. 28

3. 1958 to 1964 34

4. Redditch Carnival 67

5. The Winter of 1962/1963 74

6. Autumns 78

7. A Good Holiday and a Good Christmas 82

8. Food and Drink 1950s and 1960s 104

9. 1965 to 1970 111

10. The Fowkes Family 127

11. My Redditch 132

12. ASGO Sheet Metal Co Ltd 148

13. Radio and Television. 151

14. Significant Events 156

15. Where it Finishes! 161

Acknowledgements

I WOULD like to thank my wife, Kay, for her continued encouragement to write this book, as well as her patience whilst I was writing it. Also, thanks in particular to Peter Aston, Pauline Aston, Stuart Aston, Julie Mustafa and Jane Wormington for their ideas, inspiration and proof-reading.

Foreword

I HAD never had any intention of writing my childhood memories until I re-read my dad's own unpublished memoirs, *This is How It Was*. This was a real inspiration for me and I started to seriously consider the idea. Then, my brother Peter's wife, my sister-in-law, Pauline, followed later by my son, Stuart, suggested that it might be something that I could do, to follow on from Dad and to leave a written record of my life, or at least parts of it. This made absolute sense to me.

We all sometimes think about our ancestors' lives, how they lived on a day-to-day basis and how wonderful it would be to have some sort of record from them personally, especially at a time when genealogy activities have become so popular. So here are my childhood memories of growing up from when I was born in 1953 to when I joined the Police Force as a Cadet in 1970. I hope that you enjoy reading it as much as I have been thrilled to write it for you.

I spent a good deal of time pondering how much of my adult life I could, or might, write about. I concluded that I could possibly find myself in serious legal and security difficulties if I were to commit to paper some of those parts of my life when I was working, at one time or another, in the grey underworld of international drug trafficking, or in the deniable realms of intelligence with, or for, various UK and overseas organisations and agencies. I am sure that it might make enthralling reading but maybe not for this type of open publication, certainly not at this particular time.

I was acutely aware that, in writing these memoirs, I wanted to write about things that I remembered and how I remembered them. It would have been easy for me to just research other people's memories and to write about them but that would have defeated the object of the exercise. These are my memories of my childhood. I am sure that my brothers, Peter, a semi-professional musician and radio presenter, and Martin, will have their own and I would encourage them both, for posterity, to commit them to paper.

After reading, re-reading, amending and correcting every page of my account, I am more grateful than ever to Mum and Dad who sacrificed huge amounts to make sure that their three boys were well-fed, well-clothed and given the opportunity to truly enjoy growing up. I certainly did.

To my children, I hope that you enjoy reading the book. I would like to think that it is something that will be kept and passed on to your children then onward through future generations.

Chapter One

The Early Days – 1953 to 1958

WHERE TO start these memoirs was always going to be something of a dilemma. Everyone has a first memory of their life; something so distant and vague that they sometimes wonder whether it was a real memory, or one created from things that were related to them by others much later.

For me I can actually – I think – remember what happened. I would have been about 18 months old and living at 115 Foxlydiate Crescent in Redditch, only a bus ride from Birmingham in one direction and Worcester in the other.

My very first memory is nothing startling, more, shall we say, a natural act. I was just about toddling, and I was tottering along the linoleum floor in the living room. My mother, Jean Aston, had for some unknown reason given my age, decided that she would leave me naked from the waist down – no trousers, no plastic pants and – disastrously as it turned out – no nappy. One doesn't have to be a rocket scientist to work out what transpired. I began to deposit on the floor what would ordinarily have filled my nappy to the tune of shrieks and panic from all those present. I seem to recall that my mum's sister, Auntie Pam, was there. Anyway, I am told that the first thing to hand was the newspaper that Dad, Eddie Aston, was reading. Suffice to say that no more news was read that day!

I was born on 17th December 1953 at The Gables Nursing Home, Birchfield Road, Redditch, weighing in at 9lbs. I must say at the outset that Mum and Dad were hoping for a girl, already having had two sons, Martin and Peter. That was not to be the case, and Dad was never destined to walk a daughter down the aisle. The other, somewhat strange, thing was that, apparently, I was born with long curly hair that was bright red! Dad says in his memoirs, *"I don't remember a ginger-haired Aston ever being part of our family and I did take a good look at our milkman, but he was as dark as night!"* It seems, however, after a few weeks that my hair lost its curliness and turned much darker.

The Gables, a large house in Birchfield Road which served the town as a maternity home for many years. I was born there on 17th December 1953. Now demolished.

Seven and a half years had passed since the end of World War II in 1945 and the country, because of the conflict, remained in a state of austerity for many years with rationing still commonplace for many commodities.

Winston Churchill was the Prime Minister having been re-elected to office in 1951. The Coronation of Queen Elizabeth II had taken place in Westminster Abbey in June of my birth year, World War II hero Dwight Eisenhower was sworn in as 34th President of the USA, Ian Fleming published his first James Bond novel *Casino Royale* and Edmund Hillary, together with

Sherpa Tenzing, had conquered Mount Everest in the May. All in all, I shared my birth year with some very august people.

On the other side of the coin, I was born in the same year as convicted serial killer Rosemary West and alleged sex offender Jeffrey Epstein.

Because I arrived in the week before Christmas and new mothers, in those days, were required to be confined to bed for at least two weeks post-birth, it followed that both Mum and I celebrated our first Yuletide in The Gables Nursing Home. This necessitated some hasty festive season rearrangements for Dad, Martin, and Peter. Dad described Christmas 1953 as *"the most crestfallen, depressing Christmas I had ever had in my life!"* Peter had been shipped off to Coventry to spend the holiday period with his Auntie Win (Dad's sister), Uncle Ted and cousin, Roderick. Mum and her newborn baby (me) were in the nursing home, and he was left with Martin who had excruciating earache for the whole festive period and cried incessantly! Dad recalled the irony of four excited children from the estate arriving at the door with their Christmas Caroling, joyfully singing *"Oh Come Let Us Adore Him"* and *"We wish you a Merry Christmas."* I don't think that he felt the season of goodwill too much that year!

Foxlydiate Crescent was built between 1950 and 1953 in the Batchley area of Redditch at a time when great emphasis was being placed on post-war rehousing in the cities and large towns of the country. Batchley Estate, as it was formally named, quickly became known as "The Batchley." I must say, growing up on the estate was absolutely wonderful. Mum and Dad, with Martin and Peter, had been living in rooms in Oakly Road, near to Redditch Railway Station, but it became clear, especially as another child (me) was expected, that they needed a house of their own. They had been on the waiting list for a council house for some time and in October 1952 a letter arrived from Redditch Urban District Council saying that they had been allocated a house, 115 Foxlydiate Crescent. I don't believe that it was originally numbered 115 but, as more houses were built, house numbers were re-allocated and so 115 it became. The style of house was known as "Cornish" with concrete slabs making up the outside walls and a tiled roof that came down below the level of the upstairs bedrooms. The Astons took up residence on 12th November 1952.

Five months later, in April 1953, Mum discovered that she was pregnant – with me. On the back of this, and given that Dad was now 32 years old, he decided that he would "hang up his football boots" and end his football career. Dad had been a talented goalkeeper who had been destined for a professional career before the war broke out. He had attracted interest from top-flight clubs such as Sheffield United which, for a goalkeeper who was only around 5 feet 7 inches tall (standing on tiptoe!), was quite remarkable. Compare that with the giant goalkeepers of today and it shows just how good he was. More of his football career later.

Back to 115. This was a three-bedroom semi-detached house with a largish living room, a dining room and a kitchen. There was an indoor toilet and bathroom which, for many at that time, would have been the height of luxury. There was a large garden at the front, a long strip of lawn down the side of the house and a huge, triangular-shaped, back garden which led out onto a field – later to be built upon and become Monkspath – and then into Pitcheroak Wood. It would become central to my growing up and the scene of many imaginary skirmishes between the British and the Germans (the British would always win), between cowboys and Indians, and of tree camps, underground camps, nut and berry picking and bicycle rallying.

I lived here at 115 Foxlydiate Crescent until I was 16 years old.

The house as it stands today following extensive interior and exterior renovation.

It never ceases to amaze and disappoint me of all the things that children seem to miss out on these days, those things which we all took for granted 60 years ago. There are many reasons for that – the development of television from what used to be just two black and white channels, BBC and ITV, to the vast choice of channels available 24/7 today; the advent of personal computers and, from that, computer games; the internet; mobile telephones, tablets, the increasingly fewer places, because of building and urban development, that are available for children to invent their own imaginary worlds, and the fear factor following the massive escalation in the fear of crime against children. One could add into the mix an increasing Health and Safety culture which has led this country into becoming, in many people's eyes, an overly cautious, even a nanny, state.

I can remember, when I was three or four years old, the baker arriving in his van. He would deliver bread, stacked in a huge wicker basket, to us and our neighbours. Only plain bread, mind you, there was no such thing as sliced bread in those days. I was allowed, when the driver or the breadman as we called him, got back into the van outside our house, to close his door behind him. I used to do this regularly every week. One week, however, I missed him getting into the driver's seat and he drove off down the road. Not one to be beaten (even in those days) I chased after him down the road to where he stopped to make further deliveries with his basket. I was only a couple of hundred yards from the house but probably further than I had ever been before without anyone with me. I think that everyone on the estate heard Mum shouting at the top of her voice, *"ANTHONY!!!... Get back here NOW!"* There followed a massive telling off, many tears from me and a period of what seemed like years (probably only two days or so in reality) during which I was not allowed out of the garden.

Next door to us at 117, lived the Fowkes family, Reg and Dorothy, with their two daughters, Margaret and Jane. It must have been many years before I learned that their Christian names were Reg and Dorothy – they were only ever known as Mr. and Mrs. Fowkes. Even Mum and Dad used to call them by these more formal titles rather than by their given names but only because, in those long off times, that was normal. It was the way that things were and how neighbours addressed themselves. To the Fowkeses, Mum and Dad were Mr. and Mrs. Aston. How times have changed.

I will talk about Margaret and Jane, and of the great friendship that developed between us, in a later chapter. Suffice to say at this stage that they were a massive influence on my growing up in the Crescent and we were quite inseparable, especially during the long school summer holidays.

During those first few years, and to make ends meet, Mum took in piecework employment at home. She used to make tiny springs. Her manager, Mr. Smith (who, for some unknown reason, I used to call Mr. Muff) would deliver what looked like huge cotton reels which held extremely thin spring wire. Mum had a small spring-making gadget that bolted on to the edge of the kitchen table. It looked rather like a desktop pencil sharpener with a handle on one side and a spindle with a tiny hole in it on the other side. The wire would be slotted into the hole then the handle turned a dozen or so times to create the spring. Wire cutters were used to cut off the spring which was then thrown into a box and the process started over. Over the years Mum must have made hundreds of thousands of springs. Each week the full boxes of springs were quality-checked by Mr. Muff before being either rejected or accepted. I remember Mum telling me that, in the first few weeks, the number rejected was many more than those accepted which, she said, was somewhat soul-destroying. However, always one to persevere rather than give in, she stuck to it and, before too long, became quite a specialist. It came with something of a cost though. I described the wire as extremely thin, probably about 10 times thinner than a standard paperclip, and very sharp. Mum invariably wore sticking plasters on the end of her fingers where the wire had cut through her skin. It was, though, the added income from this work that allowed us to have a seaside holiday every summer and a lovely, present-filled, Christmas. In later years it became something of a standing joke between Peter and I that, "*We always had a good holiday and a good Christmas!*" The truth, nonetheless, was just that and we were most fortunate to have parents that did so much, and worked so hard, for their children.

On the main Bromsgrove Road, about five minutes' walk from home, and an extension of Birchfield Road, many years before the idea of Redditch New Town and the Bromsgrove Highway were even thought of, there was a Post Office which had two public rooms. One was the Post Office itself which also served as a general store and the other was a small room where you could buy tea, coffee and snacks. I think it would be stretching a point to call it a café, but it was very cosy. There were two footpaths from which you could reach the post office from the estate. One was a tarmac path that split Pitcheroak Wood in two and went past an open area of scrub land that became affectionately known as "The Patch." The other was an ash and rough stone path that meandered along the other side of the Patch. Both paths came out on the Bromsgrove Road either side of the Post Office. I vaguely remember being pushed up both paths in my pram, probably by Mum, so that she could collect her Family Allowance.

The Patch was to become the main playing area for all of us local children. Indeed, we would be most put out if any other children were found to be playing there! It was our Wembley and our Lords. We would play cup finals there and test matches. Nothing remains of it now, though, as nature has retrieved what was once hers and the raised Bromsgrove Highway runs over the top.

Just outside the Post Office was, and still is, a concrete block, about two feet in height, with a couple of steps leading up to it. This was to assist people, particularly ladies, to mount their horses in the days before motor vehicles. The block has since been converted into a small flower bed. The Post Office was to become an important part of our lives a little further down the line as, outside, it had the nearest telephone box. Very few people had private telephones then and the 'phone box became the lifeline of communication for many people, including us. It was not unusual to see people queuing outside the box waiting to use it.

The Post Office on Bromsgrove Road as a private dwelling today. The concrete block is bottom left.

The Post Office has now been converted into a private dwelling. On the other side of the road is Foxlydiate Lane. A couple of hundred yards down this lane, on the right, was another general store called Walkers. Because of this, the road was known locally as Walkers Lane. I am jumping the gun slightly because I want to tell you first about how I recall my life in the early to late 1950s in this section.

I have recollections about being admitted to hospital when I was very young. The first time was in 1955 and then again, the following year. Apparently, from the time that I was born, I had been, I am told, a very miserable baby who cried continuously for hours on end. I was taken to see the family doctor, Dr Tom Dow, who had a surgery in Worcester Road. Dr Tom was one of several family members who ended up as doctors. His father, also Tom, and brother, Ian, were doctors in the same practice. I was eventually diagnosed with not one but two hernias. However, neither of these could be operated upon until I was at least 18 months old. So, when the time came, I was admitted into Smallwood Hospital in the town centre for surgery.

Smallwood Hospital, Church Green West, where I had both of my operations.

Dr. Dow's wife was in hospital at the same time, but she was in a private ward. She had, however, taken something of a shine to me and so I was taken from the general ward and had a cot next to her in this "posh" section. Not bad for an 18-month-old! A year later I was back there having the second operation, the result of which solved the last of the hernia problems.

Dad used to have two motorcycles. Neither were particularly powerful, and I don't think he ever had both at the same time. Anyway, one was a James and other was a Royal Enfield – unsurprising as that was where Dad worked for some years. The motorbike used to live at the side of the house. Dad would use it to go to and from work and when it was parked up at home it would be covered by an old, and very heavy, tarpaulin. I can remember a hot summer before I started infant school when, in the afternoon, I would wrap myself up in this tarpaulin and fall asleep in the afternoon sun. Mum used to tell me that cats and dogs had probably peed all over it and did her best to stop me, but it was so peaceful and warm inside that I just used to love it. I expect that I would have been about four at that time. Sometimes I would lie there watching aeroplanes, propeller-driven – not jets, going overhead and which, I presume, must have been heading to and from Elmdon (later Birmingham International and now simply Birmingham) Airport. No jet vapour trails in those days, just the low drone of the engines.

At the weekend I was allowed to sit on the motorbike when it was up on its stand and I played "police bikes" for hours, wearing Dad's crash helmet, recreating verbally all the requisite sounds, the roar of the engine, changing gears, the police siren. Oh, and yes, the horn.

The horn worked without any need to have the ignition switched on so, for me, that was fair game. At best, it drove Mum and Dad nuts; at worst Dad would have a flat battery on Monday morning and would have to push-start it on the road. On a couple of occasions when I was slightly older, probably about 6, I was taken for pillion rides by Dad. There was only one crash helmet which I was given to wear. Dad would go without, which was perfectly legal in those days. One hot afternoon I was wearing shorts which was fine until I managed to touch the inside of my bare right leg onto the extremely hot exhaust pipe – not just once but twice! I ended up with a badly burned and blistered leg and Dad ended up with an earwigging from Mum when we got back home!

Many of our neighbours were already known to Mum and Dad from before they moved to 115. Redditch was a much smaller town at that time – no Woodrow, Matchborough or Winyates estates nor any other part of the New Town that would become the reality of developers' dreams years later. In fact, Webheath was only just being built at the end of the 1950s. One of these neighbours was Mrs. Hill who lived around the corner in Pine Tree

Foxlydiate Crescent in the snow.

Close. Her kitchen faced out onto the field at the back of our house and, on one afternoon, it was a good job she was at the window because she quite literally saved my life. I must have been 4 or 5 and it was nothing at that time to be allowed to wander alone in the field at the back of the house so long as I was within shouting distance.

The prequel to this story is that Martin and his friends, one of whom was Colin Hill son of Mrs. Hill and known, probably because he was rather a portly boy, as Hilly Billy, had developed a liking for building underground camps. Martin's friends mainly lived in the Crescent or Pine Tree Close: Philip Gadd, Johnny Wilkes, Jeff Perks and Michael "Mobsy" Morris. There are a couple of things that I recall about Mobsy. The first is that, in later life, he joined the Royal Marines and served in Aden during the early 1960s as part of the British Forces Aden Protectorate. The other was a couple of years earlier. Mobsy was tall and powerful. He was playing football with all the others on the Patch one weekend. Peter, poor thing, was in goal. Mobsy hit a huge shot to which Peter dived and got his arm to. Unfortunately for Peter, the shot was so hard that it bent his arm right back. Clearly in pain, Peter was not going to take any further part in the game. However, Mobsy went up to him, took his arm and shook it up and down saying, "it's only bruised!" A couple of hours, and a hospital visit later, Peter came home with a broken arm in a full plaster cast! Anyway, back to the underground camps. One or more of the lads had started digging one in this field some days beforehand. It had, however, rained heavily and the hole they had dug, which was about 8 feet deep, half filled with water. The camp digging was therefore abandoned.

Enter Anthony, stage left!

I was walking along, probably playing all sorts of imaginary games by myself, and not looking nor caring very much where I was walking, when I managed to lose my footing and fall into the water-filled hole. I could not touch the bottom, nor had I yet learned to float or swim and I can remember quite vividly, going down in the really cold water. Mrs. Hill, at the kitchen window – luckily for me – saw what had happened. She rushed into the field, shouting, and screaming. Mum heard this and also ran out to find Mrs. Hill dragging me out of the perilous watery pit. This episode, once I had been dried and recovered, was followed by yet another few days of being confined to the garden. Martin was summarily dispatched post-haste by Dad to fill the hole back in!

Batchley, at the time of building, was probably the most modern of residential estates. Today, it might not appear like that to many readers but there was, as I mentioned earlier, an inside toilet and a bathroom. Many of

The copper which served as both a washing "machine" and a water heater.

the houses in old Redditch never benefitted from such luxury. Although we had an open fire and a connected back boiler, this provided hot water only when the fire was burning. Of course, this did not help through the spring, summer and early autumn when we wanted – or more accurately, needed – a bath. We were often washed in the old Butler sink in the kitchen. Also, in the kitchen we had an old copper tub. This was a large, round metal container with a hinged lid.

It would be filled with cold water, normally using the largest saucepan that could be found, then a small gas ring underneath was lit and eventually one would have a container full of hot water. Mum would use this as a washing tub and would agitate the washing around the inside by using a large metal or wooden rod. On bath night, usually Sunday evening, it would be Dad's job to provide a copper full of hot water and to then carry it in a galvanised bucket upstairs, emptying each bucketful into the bath. This might necessitate 15 or 20 trips upstairs to get enough water in which to bathe. Being the eldest son, Martin always had the first bath followed by me and Peter who would "top and tail." Somehow, it always seemed to be me who got the taps and plug end. I invariably ended up with an indentation of the plug in my own plug end!

Bath time in the wintertime was much easier, firstly because the water was already heated by the coal fire back boiler so one could simply turn on the hot tap and secondly, when we got out of the bath, we were wrapped in a large towel that had been warmed in front of the fire and carried down to the living room, or front room as we called it, to get dry by the blazing coals.

We didn't have a refrigerator until some years later. Like all our neighbours we had a pantry, a small walk-in cupboard with shelves for tinned food and a concrete slab on which to put dairy produce or other food that had to be kept as cool as possible. Opposite this was what we called the shoe cupboard – the same size as the pantry but used to store everything for which a place could not be found elsewhere. This was essentially a junk cupboard, but the open door served as a backing for a dart board I was given one Christmas. Martin used to have his friends round some evenings for a darts competition. The number of dart holes in the back of the door were beyond counting and appeared more like woodworm!

As a small child the notion of getting the fire burning was something of an enigma. It seemed to need a whole range of things to make it work, and then a significant slice of luck. We used to have coal delivered by the coalman. He would turn up outside the house in an open-back lorry, upon which were loaded upwards of fifty heavy-duty sacking bags, each about the size of a modern-day large bin liner, and proceed to carry what had been ordered, bag by bag on his back to the coal shed, or at least the part of the shed in the back garden that was meant for coal storage. The coalman always had a black face, being covered in coal dust, a flat cap of some description, a donkey jacket which was strengthened across the shoulders and back with leather, and large, heavy boots.

Back to the fire. Mum would come down in the morning and empty the previous evening's ashes out from the grate. I say Mum because Dad would

A typical coal delivery.

have gone to work early. Having got rid of the ashes, which normally ended up becoming increasingly waterlogged by rain in a big pile at the bottom of the garden, Mum would use an old newspaper to scrunch up and use as kindling. Thin pieces of wood were placed on top of the paper, or more likely dry fir cones that we used to have to collect from the woods, followed by tiny pieces of coal then larger pieces. Incidentally, the newspaper was likely to have been the Daily Mirror. Dad was fiercely politically aligned with the Labour Party and would never entertain having a Conservative-supporting newspaper in the house. Indeed, in his younger years during World War II he says in his memoirs that he became a Communist for a period. He certainly welcomed left-wing links between Communism and the Labour Party. Until the day he died he could never bring himself to vote for any political party other than Labour.

Anyway, I digress – back to the fire, again! Normally, the first two or three attempts to get the fire to gain any strength were destined to failure and led to the consequent rebuilding of the kindling. Once the flames remained burning for any longer than five minutes Mum would get a whole sheet of the newspaper, which she had saved for the purpose, and hold it in front of the fire so that it could "draw" and thrive. It certainly did, and one could very quickly see the huge flames rising behind the sheet of newspaper – normally just before the newspaper itself caught alight and went up the chimney!

Health and Safety – 1950s style! This is how we used to get the fire going.

Anyway, it all seemed to work. Mum would then have to get coal in a bucket from the shed to leave by the side of the fire and reload it as it burned down. If we went out at all during the day, then Mum would stack the fire up with coal so that it would not go out while we were away. I don't think it ever occurred to her that the house could burn down if one of the coals rolled off, despite there being a rather flimsy-looking fireguard in place. One evening we did have to summon the Fire Brigade. Mum or Dad had got the fire burning nicely when, suddenly, there was a roaring sound from inside the chimney breast. Dad went outside to have a look at the chimney and, sure enough, there were flames licking out from the top. Someone called the Fire Brigade – we didn't have a telephone – and two tenders arrived a short time later. This was, of course, a great attraction for others in the street and so something of a crowd grew outside. All very embarrassing! The firemen quickly put the fire out and told us that the cause was the number of logs we had burned which had, over a long period of time, deposited tar and carbon on the inner lining of the chimney. The increasing temperature eventually reached a point of critical mass and ignited. It was interesting and novel to see how the firemen periodically checked to see if it was still alight. Once they had cleared out all the fire, grate, and ashes from the fireplace they placed a bowl of water in the gap. They could see from the reflection whether or not there were still flames up the chimney.

From the coal deliveries during November or December Dad would always put aside a number of large pieces of coal and not use them. "They are for Christmas Day," he told us. Later, Mum and Dad invested in having a gas pipe fed through next to the fire to which could then be connected a gas poker. It was much easier and far more successful – turn the gas on, light the poker and place it beneath the coal until the fire had well and truly caught. Later still came the addition of more luxury when we had a gas fire installed. We bought a modern Flavel Debonair. Very efficient but not much good for cooking toast or roasting chestnuts! It meant no more setting and cleaning out fires which was bliss for Mum and Dad except that we also had to have an electric immersion heater as the back boiler had to be removed as part of the installation. So, instead of just paying for coal, Mum and Dad had to fork out for more electricity. I missed the homeliness and intimacy of the coal fire, but the gas was so much cleaner and gave out instant heat.

The modern Flavel Debonair model gas fire that replaced the open fire at 115.

In the front room we had a very old and very large, dark brown leather-bound three-piece suite. I think that this used to belong to Dad's mum. It might be because I was young and small, but I seem to recall that it took up most of the room.

In the kitchen we had an old three-ring gas stove with an oven. It was made from cast iron and stood on legs. Gas in those days was "town" gas. This was gas produced as a result of burning coal and then fed to the gas holders, located off Windsor Road, a mile or so away. The gasworks consisted of two massive gas holders which were filled with gas, the pressure from which caused the holder to rise to a height of about two hundred feet. Underground pipes connected the holders to housing estates and from there to individual houses. As consumers used gas the pressure in the holders would decrease and they would sink down in a concertina fashion before being refilled again. Town or coal gas had an awful smell to it unlike, in later years, "natural" gas originating from the North Sea.

Next to the cooker was the airing cupboard, or clothes cupboard as we called it. In October and November each year this cupboard had a unique purpose. As November 5th – Bonfire Night – approached we were allowed by Mum and Dad to use our pocket money to buy fireworks from the newsagents at the top shops. The top shops were a parade of shops in Poplar Road whereas the bottom shops formed a similar parade further into the Batchley Estate near to Batchley pond. We would buy one or two fireworks, pretty ones as we were never allowed bangers, which we would take home and put in the clothes cupboard as this was the warmest and driest part of the house – it also housed the hot water tank. The Cornish houses on the estate were notorious for becoming damp during the autumn and winter, especially those walls that faced the prevailing weather. More than once, Dad lined the dining room wall with metal foil before wallpapering on top to try and prevent the damp from permeating into the house, without a great deal of success I must say though. Black and mouldy damp patches were a permanent feature through these dark and cold months. I used to check the fireworks every couple of days to make sure they were still there. Of course, they always were but, invariably, the constant lifting and checking meant that there was gunpowder residue left in the cupboard and on the clothes, but Health & Safety concerns simply didn't exist in those days, and none of us died!

The top shops at Batchley – the bus shelter in the foreground was not built until the 1980s.

Another memorable event, although not a very pleasant one, occurred when I was 5. I have always loved dogs and have, through most of my life, been lucky enough to have had some lovely canine friends.

I was playing in the front garden at Foxlydiate. It must have been late spring or summer and I was on my own. It was a hot day and so I had nothing on my top. Now, it was not unusual in those far-off days for dogs to wander around on their own sometimes strays but, more often than not, dogs where the owners had simply let them out of the house to wander wherever they chose. They would invariably return to their homes at some point during the day, probably when they became hungry.

There was a family who lived further down the Crescent who owned a German Shepherd dog, or Alsatian. I have no idea why but, as I was playing in the garden, this dog ran into our garden and jumped up at me. I don't recall whether it bit me, but my back was awash with blood where the dog's claws had dug through my skin. Looking back, I think the dog might just have been playing with me rather than attacking me but at the time it was awful – it was twice the size of me. The dog would not stop jumping up at me. Mum came out from the house as it ran off. Mrs. McDermott, who lived across the road, got her car out (she was one of the very few people who owned a car) and off we went to Smallwood Hospital. I was treated with iodine to prevent infection – which *really* stung – and patched up. From there we went to the Batchley Police House to report the matter. Police Constable Victory was on duty (coincidentally, I ended up working with him at Redditch Police Station in later years). The police house was a white-painted building near to Batchley pond and consisted of a pair of semi-detached houses both linked to a central office. PC Victory lived in one of the houses. He examined my back and took all the details as to what had happened. I was taken back home. PC Victory came to see us a couple of days later and told us that the dog's owners had been ordered to have the dog destroyed. At the time this didn't affect me untowardly but in later life that episode has haunted me somewhat because I know, through personal experience, that horrible and devastating feeling of having your dog put to sleep.

To this day, I am not convinced that the dog was being anything other than playful. Whenever I think about it, I still have huge feelings of guilt. If ever its owner's family ever get to read this book, then I am truly sorry for what happened.

Batchley Old Police House in Hewell Road.

As an aside, it was this episode that revealed that I have a significant allergy. Whilst I was at the hospital, I was given an anti-tetanus injection as a precaution. The following day my whole body expanded like a balloon, and I was covered in angry sores. Back to the hospital I was taken where I was told of my allergy to that particular medication. I have not had an anti-tetanus jab since.

Around the same sort of time, I can remember waking up one morning to the sound of what seemed to be farmyard animals outside. It turned out that a herd of about fifty cows had broken through a fence at a farm about half a mile away, wandered through the woods and down Pine Tree Close before deciding to plough their way through our, and several other, gardens. Only a small moment in life but one that I remember well, especially the smell and the mess that Dad had to clear away afterwards!

Chapter Two

Granny and Grandad – Jack and Nellie Thornton

Granny and Grandad on holiday.

THESE WERE my grandparents on Mum's side. Horrible to say, but I need to be honest from the outset. I used to dread going to see Granny! Grandad was a lovely man, but Granny always seemed to be something of a tyrant, and I was terrified of her. That said, I was looking at her purely through the eyes of a child. The reality was that here were two people who had lived through two World Wars together with the Great Depression, and raised six children, one of whom (my Mum) fell pregnant to an American GI just after the end of World War II. Hindsight is always 20:20 vision but when I look at things as they really were, I actually admire them hugely (with one exception regarding Granny which you will read about in a moment).

Grandad was called Jack even though his proper name was John, rather like US President Kennedy. He was born in Feckenham in 1892. He married Granny, Nellie Thornton née Laight, in 1916 during World War I. I was never sure why he didn't serve in the armed forces during that war. Granny was five years younger than Grandad, being born in 1897 at Crabbs Cross.

Grandad was a specialist in mending clocks and wristwatches. Even when he was in his 70s he would still mend the most intricate of watches. He was also still able to cycle up the steep Jubilee Avenue hill. Mum told me of one occasion when off he went on his bicycle with smoke and flames pouring out of his pocket. He had earlier put his, still alight, pipe in his pocket and forgotten about it until he realised he was on fire when cycling along the road!

Granny and Grandad Thornton – Wedding – Feckenham 1916.

He was the quintessential English grandfather. He would always wear a suit, with trouser braces, collar and tie, or sometimes a bow tie. Even if he was working underneath a car, he would wear a boiler suit having removed only his jacket. He smoked a pipe, had a flat cap, and loved to sit in front of an open fire, slippers on, puffing away. He was such a lovely man.

Granny had various jobs. She used to make boxes at their home, 36 Clent Avenue, Headless Cross. She had also worked in the Box Office at the Regal

Cinema which used to be in The Market Place near to the entrance to the old bus station, probably somewhere close to where the library now sits. After it was demolished, the vacant space became home to a hot dog stall.

Mum used to visit Granny and Grandad every Wednesday evening. Invariably I had to go with her. This meant catching the R22 bus from Batchley to the bus station then changing to another bus which took us to Headless Cross. We would get off the bus at the top of Jubilee Avenue then walk down the (very) steep hill to Clent Avenue. If the weather was good and it was still daylight, then I would go out, or get sent out, to play. The best part of this was that, at the junction of Clent Avenue and what is now Mansell Road, there was still an old air-raid shelter and I used to spend hours playing in that. Beyond that was a huge field, a small copse and a pond. During the summer I would pick moon daisies from there and take them back for Mum and Granny. I remember one time when I had collected what I thought was a large bunch of moon daisies. I took them to the house to be told by Granny, *"Is that all you've got. Go back and fetch some more!"* I think that Mum felt sorry for me. I felt sorry for me as well!

I mentioned that Granny made boxes. They would be things such as shoe boxes, chocolate boxes or cereal boxes, anything that required to be covered in patterned or printed paper. These would be made in the front room. This was the main living room. There was a lovely back room that housed, amongst other things, a glass fronted cabinet, the home of the "best china," but we were never allowed into this room except for special occasions. Granny would have a thick old curtain spread over the table in the front room upon which was a stack of to-be-made flat boxes and a large pot of warm glue. I can still recall the horrible, pungent smell of the glue to this day. I would sometimes hide under the table behind the curtain cover just to keep out of the way. Granny would construct the boxes then glue on the covering paper to complete the unit.

Grandad really was a lovely man, but Granny often used to shout at him and call him names. He would have been in his 60s at the time and his hands used to shake when he was carrying things, likely due to the early onset of Parkinson's disease. He would still, however, be sent to make tea in the kitchen. Subsequently, more tea would end up in the saucer than the cup and he would get into trouble for that as well.

They had a small black and white dog called Timmy. Timmy was some sort of cross terrier and Grandad used to love him. Whenever they had a cup of tea, Timmy would always be given a saucer full, including two sugars.

The family celebrating Granny and Grandad's Golden Wedding at the Foxlydiate Hotel in 1966. L-R Back Row: Me, Peter, Grandad, Uncle Bert, Martin, Auntie Pam, Uncle Eric, Auntie Lil, Uncle Bill (Price), Dad. Seated: Heather, Granny, June, Auntie Kath (Price), Mum, Great Auntie Min (Preston), Uncle Jack. Front: Hilary, Ann.

Mum and I would normally leave to go home at about half past eight and catch the buses back. Before we left, Grandad would always give me a shilling (the equivalent today of five new pence). When we got to the bus station, Mum and I would walk over to the fish and chip shop in Peakman Street and get portions to eat whilst waiting for the Batchley bus. The shop, long since demolished, was very tiny and located next to the Sportsman's Arms pub. The chips were wrapped in greaseproof paper and newspaper. Of course, newspaper ink, back in the day, was not very stable, unlike today, and once it mixed with the fat it used to run. We ended up with black marks all around our mouths and on our hands. Great taste though!

I mentioned that Mum had Martin before she met Dad just after World War II. To cut a very long story short, Martin's father, an American GI, went back to America around 1947 but wrote to Mum regularly, asking her to marry him and for her and Martin to emigrate to America. Mum never received these letters. They were intercepted by Granny who never told Mum about them. Eventually, because he received no replies to his letters, Martin's father gave up writing to Mum and no contact was ever again made between them. This is the one thing that I could never forgive Granny for. It was to be many years later, when I had grown up, before Mum found out about these letters when, of course, it was much too late. I was never sure whether Grandad knew about these letters – I suspect not.

Mum met Dad in the late 1940s when they were both working at Abel Morrall's in Edward Street and they married in 1950. It was a massive gesture on Dad's part to marry a young single mother in those times. There was such

Mum and Dad's wedding – 1st April 1950.

stigma attached to mothers bearing babies out of wedlock. I admire Dad hugely for having both the love and bravery to not care about what other people thought.

I'm afraid I don't remember anything at all about my dad's mum. She, Elizabeth Aston, died when I was still a young baby. Dad never knew his father as he died whilst his mum was pregnant with him.

Chapter Three

1958 to 1964

THE YEAR 1958 was a momentous one because it was the year that I started school. I had attained the age of 5 years in December 1958 and so I started at Batchley Infants School at the beginning of 1959.

Day one was traumatic to say the least. Because there was no such thing as nursery school, I had spent my first 5 years entirely at home with Mum. Now I was being taken to this place called school where I was going to be abandoned for hours. I said to Mum that I would not cry but as she left me at the school gates, a number of other school "virgins" were starting to cry and that set me off. It was snowing and the only way that Mum got me to stay was to promise to buy me a new pair of wellies which she would bring when she collected me that afternoon. In I went, *"creeping like a snail unwillingly to school"* (apologies to William Shakespeare's *As You Like It*).

The next problem manifested a short time later when I had been shown to my classroom and introduced to my new teacher. I don't recall her name although I remember the headmistress, Mrs. Cooper, a very strict lady with tightly curled grey hair. My teacher started talking to me and called me Tony. I said nothing. She repeated herself, still calling me Tony so again I said nothing. She started to get cross with me. I hadn't been in the building more than an hour, so this was not going at all well.

You see, Mum had always drilled it into me that my name is Anthony and that, if anyone should call me Tony, I should ignore them – so I did exactly that – all day! It was only when Mum arrived later that afternoon, armed with a brand-new pair of wellies and explained this to the teacher that matters improved immeasurably. Ironically, in my teens, I chose to be known as Tony, and have been ever since.

I spent three years at this school and really enjoyed it. There was one occasion, however, when a message was sent round to all classes that Mrs Cooper wanted to speak to all the boys after lunch because of the filthy state of the toilets. I used to go home for lunch and decided there and then that I would have a poorly tummy and not go back to school, thereby avoiding a big telling off! It worked, and I left my classmates to carry the can! I remember there being a huge assembly hall, or at least it seemed huge to me, where we used to have a religious service each morning, singing a hymn and saying a couple of prayers. When it came to saying the Lord's Prayer, Mrs. Cooper would always say *"Hands together, eyes closed"* and we would then recite it. The hall doubled up as the gym with various pieces of apparatus which were on hinges and could be rolled out onto the floor. There was a climbing frame, a rope climbing net, single ropes that went up to the ceiling and a collection of other things. There were never any safety mats at the bottom to cushion any fall, just the wooden floor. I suppose it must have taught us *not* to fall!

During my first year at the school, we didn't have any exercise books in which to write. We each had a small, wooden-framed blackboard – about the size of an A4 piece of paper – a piece of white chalk and a tiny soft board duster. This is how I learned to form letters and write – not joined-up writing though, that came later.

My second year at the school was in a class led by a young teacher, Mrs. Vaughan. Because we were now in the 2nd year, we were allowed to visit the mobile library which came to the school once a week. I was 7 years old at this stage and had started to develop an interest in reading. I had read many of the Enid Blyton series, Secret Seven, Famous Five, the Adventure series, and wanted to read other things. I found an author, Franklin W. Dixon (whom I later discovered was an umbrella name for several ghost writers), who wrote novels about The Hardy Boys. American college boys, Frank and Joe Hardy, together with their friend, Chet Morton, would solve all sorts of crimes and had lots of adventures. I had read many of the stories in books I had borrowed from Redditch Public Library. So, this was the author I sought in the mobile library. I found one, *The Yellow Feather Mystery*, and started walking back to my classroom with the booked clasped firmly in my hand when Mrs. Cooper called to me, "*What book do you have there?*" I showed her and she opened it, pointing to the word "ambitiously." She asked me what that meant but I was too scared to answer. She dismissed me abruptly saying, "*This is much too old for you. Take it back and get something else.*" So that's what I had to do. I felt so foolish.

I have no photos of me at Batchley School but here is one of Peter circa 1956 – top row, third from the right.

Another encounter with her was when I had raging earache one day. I did not know where to put myself. I had been weeping in class, so I was sent to sit in Mrs. Cooper's office. I'm not sure how this was meant to ease my pain, but Mrs. Cooper kept shouting at me, telling me to stop crying. I didn't. She was another woman who terrified me. It turned out that I had somehow developed a perforated ear drum which was causing incredible pain. Thankfully, this led to me having a few days off school while it was treated. It never completely mended though and remains to this day.

At that time, and maybe it still does, Batchley School had a huge playing field, which backed onto the back gardens of houses in Cherry Tree Walk and Willow Way. Weather permitting, we used to take full advantage. On the field there was a large fallen tree which must have lain where it had fallen years earlier – I can't imagine anyone having reason to drag it there. We called this "the log" and we spent hours of our playtimes on it. It would be a boat, a spaceship, a submarine, or just somewhere to sit – it could be anything that we wanted it to be, but it was ours. The field itself was massive – or seemed to be at least – but of course, periodically, the grass needed cutting. This involved the visit of a local farmer on his tractor with a grass-cutting piece of machinery towed behind. This was wonderful because it meant that we could have grass fights! Also, it would not be unusual for the tractor to be cutting during playtime and dinner time. We would often follow it around the field, picking up and throwing copious amounts of grass as we went. If it came towards us we simply moved out of the way. Teachers didn't scream at us, nor did they keep us indoors until the tractor had left the school. And parents didn't make any complaints to the school when they learned how we had been playing alongside the tractor. This was all part of growing up for us and, once again, no-one died!

At the bottom of the playing field was a small pond. This was ordinarily out-of-bounds to all of us children but sometimes we were taken down there as part of nature lessons. I can remember having to bring a jam jar from home so that we could collect frog spawn. The jars, full of spawn and pond water, were kept in the classroom and we would look at them every day to see when the spawn developed into tadpoles. Once they had started to grow and lose their tails, we would trot off again to the pond and release them back into their natural surroundings.

The school had, from a local garage, managed to procure a whole load of used car and lorry tyres which we were allowed to roll around the field at will during playtime and dinner breaks. Yes, they hurt if they rolled into you but, again, one simply learned to jump out of the way. We would also play games such as leapfrog and British bulldog, games that might well be, and probably are in many schools, banned today. Bulldog in particular was a very physical game. There were two teams, and the idea was that one team had to run and break through the lines of the second team. It was up to the second team to stop them which would involve tripping, dragging or pushing them to the floor – any means to stop the line from being breached. Cuts and bruises were commonplace but all part of the game. Imagine that today! In the autumn we played conkers (without, I might add, safety goggles and gloves!). Conkers were readily available from horse chestnut trees in September and October. Having collected dozens, I would select the biggest as my playing conkers. This involved drilling a small hole through the conker from one end to the other and threading string or a shoelace through. Tying a knot in one end so that the conker didn't fall off, you were ready for action. You would take turns with your opponent to break his conker with yours, and vice versa. If you broke his then your conker became a "oner." After two victories it became a "twoer" and so on. However, if your opponent's conker was already graded, for instance, a "sixer" then these six would be added onto yours when you had smashed his. This was a great game but one riddled with opportunities of gamesmanship, such as "accidentally" bringing your conker down with force onto the opponents unprotected knuckles! It was also something of an artform to move your conker just slightly as your opponent brought his down. Not enough whereby you could be accused of deliberately cheating, but just enough so that, at worst, your conker only received a glancing blow rather than a full-on strike. If the strings became entwined with each other after a shot then the first player to shout "tangle, tangle one two three" won a free hit.

On the playing field there used to grow what we called vinegar leaves. I had no idea at the time what they were called but we used to eat them because they tasted, well, just like vinegar. We loved them. A little research has revealed that these were Common Sorrel leaves that grow close to the ground, are not poisonous (verified by the fact that I am still here 60 odd years later writing these memoirs) and could be used in cooking.

It was at Batchley School in my third and last year when I was introduced to playing football by my teacher Mr. David. I think he must have lived in the Bromsgrove area as I would see him every morning walking down Pine Tree Close from the direction of where the Bromsgrove bus would have dropped him. I had a pair of football boots that Dad had found from somewhere. The studs were made from leather and had nails protruding from the base. A hammer was used to affix the studs to the bottom of the boots. I don't recall much about the games that I played but I must have enjoyed it as it was something I played for many years afterwards.

My teacher in the last year at Batchley was Mrs. Timmis. Coincidentally, her husband worked as a teacher at Holyoakes Field Junior School to which I moved when I finished at Batchley. She was a lovely and kind woman, very different to how I remember her husband, and we got on really well. One of my favourite activities, which she always let me help with, was clearing up the store cupboard.

My best friend at Batchley School was Christopher Cordwell. He lived at the other end of Foxlydiate Crescent, No. 5 I think, which was very close to the school. I used to call for him on my way in. I also used to go to his house to play sometimes.

Me and Peter in the front garden at 115 Foxlydiate Crescent circa 1963.

One morning we were walking to school together on a day on which we must have been due to play football. I say this because I recall having my boots with me. I remember this particular day because I was swinging my boots over my head by the laces, something which Mum had always told me not to do. Of course, the inevitable happened. One of my boots connected full on with Chris' nose. Lots of screaming from him, understandably, blood streaming from his nose and neighbours rushing out to see what had happened. He went running off back home, but I had no choice other than to carry on to school. I was asked by the teacher where Chris was but all I could say was, *"I don't know!!"* He turned up a little later with a huge swollen nose that was stuffed with cotton wool. Sorry didn't seem to cut any ice with him but he forgave me later.

Mum used to excel at baking and cooking except, that is, when it came to Yorkshire puddings. She used to make one large one rather than several small, but it always came out as flat as a pancake! I'm sure my love of cooking came from Mum. She taught me so much. The best days were those when she would bake a cake. Now this had nothing to do with the final product. It was all about getting her to leave as much of the cake mix in the bowl as I could persuade her to do so that I could scrape the bowl. There is nothing quite like the taste of cake mix. Me and Peter would be given the bowl and we would both have a teaspoon to transfer the goodies into our very welcoming mouths. Of course, it was inevitable that I would encroach on Peter's "half," or he into mine, but it would somehow work. I tell you what, the bowl would need no washing after we had finished with it! This would be augmented by a sneaky dip of the finger into the mix that was in the baking tin before it was put into the oven. This reminds me of the chips that Mum used to cook. Like most families, we had a chip pan that lived on the stove and, when not being used, was half full of solidified lard. No vegetable oil in those days. If we were to have chips with our dinner, then Mum would heat up the lard in the pan on the gas ring until it was boiling. She would put the freshly sliced potatoes into the chip basket and lower it into the fat. Five or six minutes later we would have the best chips ever, outside of those from the chip shop, crisp on the outside and soft in the middle. Even better was if they were going to end up inside chip butties!

There are certain smells that evoke childhood memories too. Freshly mown grass always reminds me of Dad (and me when I was a little older) mowing the lawns at Foxlydiate with a manual lawnmower, Qualcast I think. I can't remember when I last saw one of those, except in a museum. Mind you, I used to loath being given the job of trimming the borders with a pair of not very sharp garden shears! Whenever I smell cut grass these days it takes me straight back to those days.

Another smell is that of hot road tar. This was in the days when roads would be resurfaced every 3 or 4 years. It always seemed to take place in the summer, and it was in the days when local authorities would resurface the whole road, not just the deepest holes! It always strikes me as a little odd that roads were completely and regularly resurfaced when there was comparatively very little traffic on the roads as opposed to today when you're lucky if potholes get filled at all but there is massively more traffic using the highways. A bizarre sort of progress, I suppose. Anyway, the day would come when the stretch of road outside our house was due for resurfacing. Firstly, the old surface would be scored, and all loose bits removed. Then the hot tar went down, poured from a machine at the back of a lorry. Each side of the road was done separately. Almost immediately, another lorry would drive down the unprepared side and two men on the back would shovel stone chippings onto the hot, wet tar. Another man would rake it level and then the road-roller would come along and flatten the road level with its huge metal roller wheels. Originally, the road-rollers were steam-driven but steam in the 1950s was on its way out and later rollers were diesel-powered. Once this had been achieved the other side of the road would be done whilst traffic used the "new" side. At the end of the day, when the road was completely finished, we would be out playing on it. Because cars and lorries were few in number in those days, the road was a natural playground for us. The only problem, it transpired, was that tar that was still tacky would get onto our clothes and shoes, then get walked into the house. I can still hear Mum shouting "GET YOUR SHOES OFF!" to us.

Another smell I remember is that of a blowtorch being used by council workers to burn the old paint off the house doors and windows ready for a fresh coat. All the doors in the road would be painted with the same colour. Again, this would happen every four or five years. I don't think local authorities ever do that these days but maybe that is because councils and housing associations have replaced wooden doors with UPVC, as well as the inherent cost.

When I finally left Batchley School I went to Bridge Street Junior School, which had just changed its name to Holyoakes Field School. Getting to the school in the morning entailed catching the school bus from Batchley which dropped us off at the school gates. This got quite boring after a while and it was no coincidence that the pedestrian bridge that crossed the local railway line was next door to the school (hence the name, Bridge Street). Rather than catch the school bus I would catch the earlier public one and get off in Hewell Road at the bottom of Bates Hill (before the road railway bridge I hasten to say but I will explain about that later). It was then a short walk down an alley from Windsor Street across the pedestrian railway bridge which crossed the main Redditch to Birmingham line next to Redditch Railway Station. If I timed it correctly, I would meet my friends around 8 o'clock and we would wait on the bridge for the 8.10am steam train to leave the station and travel directly underneath where we were standing.

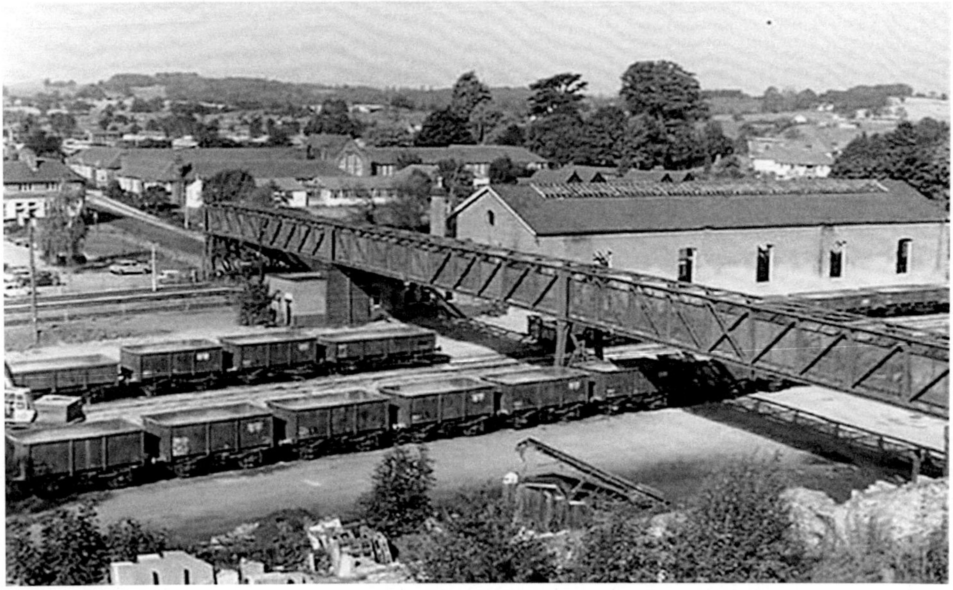

The railway footbridge upon which I would stand as the early morning team train left Redditch Station. Holyoakes Field School is in the background.

The thrill of the engine and the smell of the steam mixed with smoke was second to none. This quickly became a daily ritual, as did the dressing down from teachers and Mum because the nice, clean, white shirt, smart grey shorts and blue jumper always ended up as a nice, grey/black shirt with shorts that were even greyer and a bluey/grey jumper. Of course, we ignored the ensuing ban on walking across the bridge but the state of our skin and clothes well and truly gave us away.

It was probably around this time that I first started noticing black people in the town. The 1950s and 1960s heralded a huge influx into the UK of first-generation immigrants from the Caribbean Islands. Redditch was no exception and I suddenly started to see black conductors on the buses and black women out shopping. This was something of a novelty to me. I had never seen black people before and I must admit to often staring at them. Many of them would take up residence in the Oakly Road area of Redditch which is close to the Railway Station, and they would paint their doors and window frames in bright colours. They had come here to help the British economy, to boost the workforce – there were many more job vacancies than people to fill them at that time – and to make a better life for themselves and their families. It is no secret, however, that these mainly West Indian, immigrants were often verbally and physically abused. Even in primetime TV shows such as *'Til Death Us Do Part,* they were referred to in derogatory terms. How arrogant and insulting we were back then. Such language is rightly not tolerated today but, as children of the era, we would chant rhymes such as *"Eeny, meeny, miney mo, catch a nigger by his toe, if he squeals let him go, eeny, meeny, miney, mo"* without giving any consideration or thought whatsoever to what we were actually saying, nor to the hurt, anger and offence that the words must have generated. The film industry of the time did little to exempt itself from similar language allusions. For instance, In the 1955 movie *The Dambusters* the black pet Labrador dog of Wing Commander Guy Gibson was called "Nigger". Indeed, the dog's grave at RAF Scampton in Lincolnshire to this day bears its name and inscription.

So, I am now at Holyoakes Field School which, as I write these memoirs, is due for demolition. The school was renamed after Sir Keith Jacka Holyoake, the Prime Minister and Governor-General of New Zealand. I have no idea why so maybe a reader will be able to solve this little mystery. The year was 1961 which in itself is an interesting kind of number. It is one of those whereby

Holyoakes Field School, photo courtesy of Elliott Brown.

if you turn it upside down it remains the same number. This was discussed on the TV in *Blue Peter* at the time (presented by Christopher Trace and Valerie Singleton) and I learned that this type of number is called *strobogrammatic*.

My first teacher was Mrs. Greenacre. She was a very kind lady. I remember some of the children who were in my year – Kevin Ireland, Sheila Chambers, Heather Baker, Christopher Cordwell (of course), Margaret Carson, Lynette Jones (who lived on a farm in Brockhill Lane), Ian Geddes (son of a local vet), Andrea Walker, and many others, all of whom will no doubt have their own stories to tell. Another friend, Martyn Lolley, was in one of the neighbouring classes but, even at a young age, was a brilliant footballer whom, I believe, went on to play at semi-professional level. Anecdotally, his son Joe, at the time of writing, is a professional footballer with English Championship club, Nottingham Forest.

I went to Ian Geddes' house to play one day. He lived in a big, detached house on Bromsgrove Road near to the town centre. We played in his back garden and started throwing small stones to see who could throw the furthest. I threw mine and a second or two later we heard the very distinct sound of breaking glass. I had, unintentionally but successfully, found the greenhouse! Ian told his mother who came out and said "Anthony, I think you had better go home now!" I was never invited back. Mrs. Greenacre's son was also at the school but younger and in a different class to me. He used to get a whole load of verbal stick from other pupils; teacher's pet, snitch etc. Children can be so cruel, and I look back with no pride in taking part in some of that which, these days, would be considered as bullying.

The school was divided into three parts – infants, juniors, and seniors. Because I had already attended Batchley Infant School I started off in the juniors. There was a huge playground which was divided down the centre by a brick wall that was about 3 feet (1 metre) high with gaps at either end to walk through. Infants and juniors were confined to one side while the seniors (aged 10 or 11) ruled the roost on the other side. They had the use of a climbing frame which we were not allowed to use. There were only certain occasions when we were allowed into the Juniors playground. The location of the school back entrance/exit meant that at the beginning and end of the day we had to walk through that way. Also, the outside toilet block was located in the junior section.

Outside toilets are not great at the best of times but certainly not in the winter, often freezing up. We had to trudge across there in all weathers to do what we had to do. The smell was often overpowering and the floors usually wet where either the roof had leaked, or boys had missed with their aim. Other unforgettable odours were those of school disinfectant and carbolic soap – never to be forgotten. The worst experience, though, was the use of Izal toilet paper – very rough on one side and smooth on the other. Using it often meant getting really sore or ending up in more of a mess than when you started!

Occasionally, we would see the school caretaker. He would be the one who would change lightbulbs and mend things. What I remember him for more than anything, however, is that he was the one who, if someone had been sick on the floor, would come in with a bucketful of sawdust to soak up the mess. This would not be a quick job and the sawdust would have to be left for an hour or more to make sure that everything had been absorbed. Another unmistakable stench!

We used to go to the class next door for English lessons with Mr. Johnston. He was ordinarily a very cheery, funny man and we enjoyed his lessons. He had, however, a temper which when he lost it would involve ranting and raving often coupled with throwing objects at children ranging from chalk to books to wooden board dusters (imagine *that* these days!). On one occasion, Mr. Johnston – unbeknown to us – must have been having a really bad day. We all entered the classroom, shouting and yelling and he lost it, screaming at us, "*WOULD YOU LOT BEHAVE LIKE THIS IN MRS. GREENACRE'S CLASS?!*" Enter Anthony with my big mouth. "Yes, we would!" I shouted. I was hauled out in front of the class, all of whom were by this time totally silent and more than happy to let me carry the can. "Well, go next door into Mrs. Greenacre's class right now and start shouting and playing up like you were just then!" At that I was thrown, bodily, from his classroom. The rest of the class waited with bated breath to hear the noise that I was going to have to make when I walked into my teacher's class. I waited and waited until Mr. Johnston came out and shouted "Well, go on then." I started to cry and blubbered "I don't want to!" He gave me a "thwack" with his hand across both ears and ordered me back into his class with instructions to "sit down and don't make another sound." I didn't!

I used to enjoy physical education for which we used the hall. This would often include the broadcasting of a radio programme called "Music, Movement and Mime" from a loudspeaker contained in a huge wooden housing. We exercised to this – great fun.

At the end of the day, 4 o'clock, one of us children would be deployed to go into the centre of the playground taking with us quite a large hand-bell. The bell was rung which signalled to all pupils that home time had arrived. There would be a mass exodus from classrooms into the cloakrooms for coats and bags and everyone disappeared within minutes. Ordinarily I would catch the school bus home. This picked us up directly outside the school in Bridge Street itself. Sometimes, however, I would either walk home or use Peter's bicycle which I occasionally "borrowed" from him.

On one occasion at school, when we were with Mr. Johnston, the home bell went but he said nothing. A minute or so went by before someone (not me!) put their hand up and said, "Excuse me, sir, the bell has gone" to which he looked up and after a moment's consideration, said with a sigh, "They'd take anything around here!" We were then let out.

On Wednesday morning each week we would be taken, walking in double file, to Redditch Swimming Baths in Hewell Road, a distance of about a quarter mile. We all carried our swimming gear rolled up in a towel. This is where I was taught to swim. Once you had managed to swim a width of the pool you received a red cotton stripe that was sewn onto your swimming trunks. Swimming a length got you a yellow stripe. A green stripe was given to those who could swim a length then, with pyjamas on, dive or jump into the water and retrieve a heavy rubber block from the bottom.

Sometimes, when the weather was good, I would walk to school. This took about half an hour. I would walk along Bromsgrove Road to the start of a hill by the Queens Head Pub. Opposite, there was a laundry which had a narrow footpath leading to a playing field next to Redditch Town Football Club (it would not become Redditch United for many years). From here another path took me through allotments and emerge by the school entrance. I can't imagine that young children would be allowed to walk alone through those lonely paths these days, that is, if they still exist.

We were lucky enough to get school trips several times a year. One time we went to Coughton Court, about half an hour away by coach. I was allowed

On the way to Coughton Court – Brownie 127 camera around my neck circa 1963. Photo taken in Bridge Street with Edward Street on the right and the railway footbridge in the background where I used to get covered in soot and smoke.

to take the family Brownie 127 camera and I remember using up the whole film, a total of 8 photos that the film allowed. I don't recall how many were successful but older readers will remember taking the used roll of film into Boots the Chemist then waiting for a week or more before the photographs and negatives could be collected. Another time, we were taken to visit Quinney's Farm, a local dairy in Sambourne, a small nearby hamlet. Quinney's was the main provider of fresh milk in the Redditch area for many years. The sound of the electric milk floats driving along the road and the clinking of milk bottles being delivered onto doorsteps were the most reassuring of sounds that broke the early morning silence.

When I became a senior I "crossed the playground" and became a part of Mrs Turner's class. She was a very firm lady who must have been approaching retirement. She lived in Clent Avenue, Headless Cross quite close to Granny and Grandad. She ruled with a rod of iron in the classroom and had a habit of bringing children out in front of the class if they had done something wrong or if their work was not up to the expected standard. She would start shouting at whomever was unfortunate enough to be stood there. This would be followed by her continually bashing them on the back with the flat of her hand. Some children would seem to be subjected of this treatment more than others. I felt very sorry for them but at the same time I was glad it wasn't me.

Towards the end of the school year in the Juniors we were taken on a trip over three days to London. Mr. Simpson and Mrs Turner were the lead teachers and off we went in a coach. Mum gave me the usual barley sugar boiled sweets to suck on if I felt sick on the coach. I didn't but the sweets still disappeared. I enjoyed this trip so much right up until the moment that we were travelling back to Redditch but more of that in a moment.

We went around many of the usual sights in the city – Buckingham Palace, Whitehall, various museums – and I loved every minute of it. I had never been to London and so experiencing all the hustle and bustle, travelling on

School picture at Holyoakes Field School circa 1964.

the underground railway and just the general feel of being in the Capital, left a lasting impression on me.

We stayed at a hotel in Russell Square. I seem to remember it was called the Royal. This was early in 1964 at a time when the Swingin' Sixties was indeed in full swing. The Beatles seemed to be perpetually at the top of the charts, other pop groups were there or thereabouts, and for girls the mini skirt seemed to rule.

One morning, some of the other children, mainly girls, started banging on my room door. It seemed that a new band called "Them" were staying at the same hotel a few floors higher. They had a hit in the charts called "Here Comes the Night." I'm not sure how we found it but off we went and knocked on the door of this room. It was opened by a man who had very long hair, was wearing jeans and nothing on his top. Someone plucked up the courage to ask for autographs and the band promptly obliged. I had no paper, just a small leather zip-up purse so I offered this for signature. Back in my room I looked at all the signatures and the only one I could read was someone called Ivan Morrison, which meant absolutely nothing to me. Apparently, he was the band's lead singer. I lost the purse, or threw it away, sometime later little knowing that I had just got, and lost, the autograph of the now legendary rock star, Van Morrison.

On the last evening we were taken to the Whitehall Theatre to watch comedy actor Brian Rix in one of his farces. This was like nothing I had ever been to before. Brian Rix was, of course, famous for dropping his trousers during the performance. This seemed so naughty to us "country bumpkins" and we laughed until we cried.

The following morning, we were due to leave for home and this is where things somewhat fell apart for me.

On my first birthday I was given a teddy bear by Auntie Pam. He was called simply "Teddy" and he went everywhere with me. To this day he has pride of place on a corner unit of our living room. He also went to London with me, which, for an eleven-year-old boy, was not a piece of information that I wanted to share with anyone else for fear of ridicule.

On that last morning we had breakfast with most children having packed their suitcases beforehand. I, of course, had not and so it was all a bit of a rush afterwards to get packed and take my case down to reception.

A little later we all boarded the coach and waited whilst the obligatory headcount was carried out by Mrs. Turner. Mr. Simpson was the last to board and he had a number of things in his hand. He had checked all rooms and collected those items that had accidentally been left behind. There were socks and a shirt that were handed to their owners and people giggled. Then, to my horror, he held up a teddy bear, *my* Teddy, and said, "And who does this teddy bear belong to?" At that moment I hated him because he knew full well from whose room he had collected it. I felt completely humiliated as I had to put my hand up with everyone laughing and pointing at me. It was a dreadful moment and I began to sob. To my rescue, and I saw a very different side of her in that moment, came Mrs. Turner. She took Teddy from Mr. Simpson and gave him a look that could have killed.

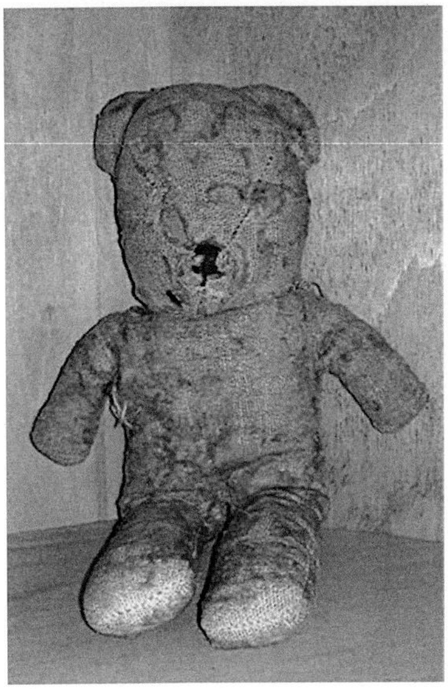

Teddy today – 66 years old – who now lives on display in my living room

She sat down next to me, put her arm around me and genuinely comforted me. I loved her for that and even more, later in the journey, when she gave Mr. Simpson a real and very sharp, verbal dressing down. I half expected her to start banging him on the back. This was done very quietly in the front seats of the coach, but I was not seated far away, and I heard her. I don't believe that Mr. Simpson ever repeated anything so insensitive. He never spoke of it to me ever again. For my part, after that I never had a bad word to say about Mrs. Turner.

Just down the road from the school, in Hewell Road, was a factory called Renown Springs. Mum worked there for a few years and sometimes I would walk home that way rather than catch the school bus and wave to Mum and her friend, Edna Poyner. They both worked on the top floor but always had the window open.

Edna took a bit of a shine to me and it was lovely when, one weekend, she and her husband took me to Gaydon Air Show in Warwickshire. I had never been to an air show before and to see jets such as the English Electric Lightning and Vulcan bombers screaming through the sky was both unforgettable and breath-taking.

Outside of school, I remember that Mum and Dad would sometimes go to the Brockhill pub for a drink. These days the building is still there but is now occupied by Tesco supermarket. It is situated next to the bottom shops near to Batchley pond in Willow Way, not far from Batchley School. In the summer Peter and I would sometimes go along with them, and we would sit on the wall outside with a bottle of Vimto and a packet of crisps. Children were completely barred from pubs in those days.

The benefit of Mum and Dad drinking here was that, at Christmas, we were able to go to either a Birmingham or Coventry theatre with loads of other children whose parents were patrons of the Brockhill, or the "Brock" as it was known, to see a pantomime. I recall seeing stars of the day such as Frank Ifield and Cilla Black in various productions and thinking how wonderful it must be to be famous. The pantomime would follow a regular pattern. The star of the show would play a lead part which would often be a hard-done-by character but who ended up being the hero of the day. The star would come onto the stage after the panto had finished and sing several of their hit songs. Looking back, we were so lucky. Many of my friends never had this opportunity.

A Christmas treat from the Brockhill Pub.

A really sad part of my life occurred around this time when Mum suffered what today would be referred to as mental illness but what was then simply called a mental breakdown. I was not old enough to understand, although I was of an age to know that something was very wrong with Mum. She had to go away for a few weeks to Barnsley Hall near Bromsgrove. Barnsley Hall was built in Victorian times and, for many years, was a residential mental asylum, part of which housed a secure unit. Even now, I am not fully aware of the ins and outs as to why Mum ended up there, but I know that she received what was commonly referred to as "electric shock treatment."

The mental health organisation MIND describes this as *"ECT (Electroconvulsive Therapy), a treatment that involves, under general anaesthesia, sending an electric current through the brain to trigger an epileptic seizure to relieve the symptoms of some mental health problems."* It is a treatment that is not commonly used today but many years ago it was implemented routinely. It must have been awful for Mum and Dad to have to go through this. Mum must have made something of a good recovery because she was discharged at some point and never, as far as I know, had to return to the Hall although Peter seems to recall that perhaps she did. I don't remember it ever being spoken about in the family.

One of the highlights of that last year at the school was the Christmas Carol Service. This was organised and run by Mr. Timmis, whom I mentioned earlier.

He never seemed to be a very friendly individual. Early in November he would select all the children who were going to be in the school choir. I was lucky enough to be chosen. Each one selected was given a booklet which contained all the words for the carols that would be sung at the Service. We were expected to learn all of these off by heart and we had weekly practice sessions in school.

The Service itself was always held on a Friday night, in early December, inside Bates Hill Methodist Church, a short walk of about 10 minutes from the school. This was a beautiful building at the top of the hill but which, sadly, was later demolished following a major fire.

The week before the Service we had a dress rehearsal in the church. I remember this going quite well until Mr. Timmis called out to one of the boys, Paul, a rather small, befreckled, carrot-haired boy who lived in Pine Tree Close. Unfortunately for him, he had not bothered to learn or had forgotten, the words to several carols. He was hauled to the front of the church balcony and told to sing a particular carol on his own with the rest of the choir watching. Of course, not knowing the words he couldn't do this, and Mr. Timmis shouted at him: *"You have not learned any of the words. You are a disgrace to the school, and you are out of the choir. Go and sit downstairs!"*

To not be part of the choir was a massive blow as all parents, family and friends would be at the Service – the church was capable of sitting several hundred people and it would be packed on the night.

I am not sure what transpired over the ensuing days nor what conversations, heated or otherwise, might have been held between Mr. Timmis and the new headmaster, Mr. Etheridge, but suffice to say that a few days before the Service went live, Paul had learned all the words and was back in the choir.

All traditional carols were included, and I was asked if I would sing one of the verses of "*We Three Kings*" on my own. I was terrified but said that I would. This meant that instead of just sitting up in the balcony with the rest of the school I, and the other soloists, had to climb a very dark, narrow staircase behind the huge organ and through a tiny "Judas Gate" to get to a row of seats that really were up in the Gods. The congregation down below seemed so tiny, but I sang my heart out for that verse:

Myrrh is mine
Its bitter perfume breathes A life of gathering gloom,
Sorrowing, sighing, bleeding, dying,
Sealed in the stone-cold tomb.

Three years before my famous solo, Peter had also been in the choir and gave a solo rendition of the first verse of *Once in Royal David's City* as the choir entered the church.

I think he was quite nervous, and I remember Mum threatening me before we arrived there. I was banned from looking at him and making him laugh!

I recall having a recurring nightmare for many years as I was growing up. If I had been naughty (quite often!) then I would be sent to my bedroom as a punishment. After a while I would sit on the top of the stairs and shout downstairs, asking if I could come down yet. The answer was often, no. Eventually I would be allowed back down but not before much sobbing and tears. I don't remember the exact moment when they started but I began to have this nightmare dream. I would be upstairs in our house, and I would walk into either my room or Mum and Dad's. I had this growing dread that "something" was there that wanted me to stay upstairs so that it could grab me. I never discovered what this "something" was, but it was certainly nothing very

The very imposing Bates Hill Methodist Church.

pleasant and I would try to run downstairs to escape. My arms and legs would feel as though they were attached to strong elastic, and I would never be able to make it downstairs. Whatever "it" was, was dragging me back up the stairs no matter how hard I struggled to get free. As I got closer and closer to the top of the stairs I would start to scream, resulting in me waking up, terrified. This nightmare must have gone on until my mid-teens, but it changed subtly over the years. As I got older, I became stronger both physically and mentally. It got to a point in the nightmare where I was able to reach the bottom of the stairs and escape. As I got older still, I found myself going back up the stairs of my own accord to confront whatever it was that had been after me for years. Even now I will have versions of this dream. I expect a good psychologist would be able to write a whole after-dinner speech about my nightmare!

Batchley had its own church, St David's, a small pre-fabricated affair that was built after World War II and demolished in the 1980s.

Both Peter and I used to go to Sunday School there in the later 1950s. There was also a mid-week youth club that Peter would attend more than me because he was that much older.

We would not always go to Sunday School together, sometimes I would go on my own. Mum would give me thruppence (three old pennies) for the collection. I need to tell you two things, one linked with the other. Firstly, every child was given what was effectively a stamp album and, each week at Sunday School, we would be given a stamp to lick and put in our album. Each stamp bore a different religious picture. If you didn't attend, you didn't get the stamp for that week which meant that you would not be eligible for a "perfect attendance" prize at the end of each year. Secondly, sometimes I would not go to Sunday School. Oh, I would get my Sunday best on and head off clutching my collection money, but I wouldn't go, and I would spend the money on sweets, returning home at the appropriate time. This ruse worked quite well except for the fact that I did not get my stamps for the weeks that I missed so not only would I not get a prize, but Mum and Dad would work out that I hadn't been attending. This situation needed to be resolved.

Now, even at that age, I could be quite an astute little fellow. I persuaded Mum to let me go to the youth club mid-week for the first hour and then come

I am not in this photograph, but it is the only one I could find of St David's Church, Batchley.

back. She agreed, and I think she was quite pleased that I had taken such an interest in the church.

I must admit to feeling more than a little ashamed because whilst at the youth club I worked out where the vicar, Reverend John Fearn (I will tell you more about him in a moment), kept all the old stamps that were left over. It was quite a simple task then to take the stamps missing from my book and to stick them in to show evidence of my "perfect attendance." I could also purloin stamps for forthcoming weeks because they were kept in the same box. I managed to win attendance prizes for three years in a row – I can't think how! The things that you do as children... but another that, once again, I am not proud of today.

The Reverend John Fearn was the vicar at St David's Church for several years. He used to ride a motorcycle that had a sidecar attached in which I had a ride once. I was taken poorly one Sunday, and he gave me a lift home. Anyway, he left in 1964 to become the new vicar at a small place called Bladon in Oxfordshire. Little did he know that only a few months later he would be one of the clerics officiating at the burial of Sir Winston Spencer Churchill at the family grave at Bladon Church following the funeral service earlier that day at St Paul's Cathedral in London. I remember seeing him during the television broadcast. What also sticks in my memory from television coverage that day is, when Churchill's coffin was being taken down the River Thames, all the construction cranes on the riverbanks were lowered in remembrance and commemoration of this most revered of men.

Many Saturday afternoons I would spend watching Redditch Town Football Club playing at the Valley Stadium which used to be down a very steep track off Bromsgrove Road. I think it cost sixpence to get in and another thruppence to buy a programme. In the 1960s Redditch Town, years before they became Redditch United, played in the West Midlands (Regional) League. The ground was very basic. There was an old wooden stand, which these days would probably have been condemned, it cost an extra thruppence to go in and sit down. To avoid payment, I would often try to sneak in at half-time. Behind both goals were grass banks, which became very muddy during the winter, and on the opposite side to the stand was a corrugated iron covered terrace which had seen much better days. Immediately behind this was the Cedar Road bungalow to which Margaret and Jane Fowkes had moved to when they left the Crescent – more of them in another chapter.

Half-time would always follow the same ritual. A trip to the almost primitive.... no, actually, it *was* primitive... toilet which consisted of a pit dug into the ground which housed several old oil barrels with the tops removed, then a plank of wood across the top of each with holes created which sat over the top of each barrel. Not a very pleasant experience and the smell was unbearable. Goodness knows who had the job of digging out the contents to empty it. This was followed by the purchasing of a hot cup of Bovril and a Wagon Wheel chocolate biscuit from the tiny café. This was a real treat although, as I remember them, Wagon Wheels were much bigger back then than they are today!

Occasionally, Peter and I would visit my dad's sister, Auntie Mabel, who lived in the "steel houses" on the Mayfields Estate. They were called steel houses because the vertical claddings on the top half of the houses were made of steel. She lived with Uncle Ken and my cousins Sue and Warwick. One thing I remember about these visits, especially if Mum had left us there for the day, was that Auntie Mabel used to make her own faggots. Faggots were made from cheap offcuts of meat, bound with cereal, and wrapped in caul or

25 Sycamore Road, Mayfields where Auntie Mable, Uncle Ken, Sue and Warwick lived.

kell. This was the part I never liked. Caul or kell is a membrane from a pig's abdomen and used to hold each faggot together. I remember pushing my faggot to and fro along the plate trying to separate the meat, which I loved, from the wrapping. Auntie Mabel could never understand why I didn't like it, but I always managed to leave it on the side of my plate.

Back to school and this was a time when many of Britain's rural railway lines were at risk of being closed as what became known as the "Beeching Axe," a reference to the then Chairman of the British Railways Board, Dr Richard Beeching, whose report led to many such closures. Redditch was no exception and the line south of Redditch leading to Evesham had already been closed. The line to Birmingham in the other direction was also earmarked for closure. The school organised a trip to Redditch railway station to gauge the opinion of the workers there. They gave their opinion in no uncertain terms, and in language that I could not possibly repeat here, and which the teachers with us never expected to hear! Our class then had a debate in the classroom about the closure. One of the class, David Brazier, son of a local photographer, chaired the meeting and wore his father's bowler hat. At this time, and totally separate to anything to do with railways, there was a television campaign from the Egg Marketing Board to promote British eggs. Their slogan was *"Go to work on an egg."* David came up with an alternative slogan for us, *"Don't go to work on an egg, go by train!"* I don't know whether we had any influence, but the final decision was that the line to Birmingham would remain open and is still running to this day.

Towards the end of my last year at Holyoakes Field, it was time for me to sit the dreaded 11+ examination. This was all part of the selection process as to who would move on to Grammar School and who would be sent to Secondary Modern Schools. I was 11 years old and had no idea of the importance of this exam and in which direction it might take my life.

I had never taken a "real" examination before, only tests of one sort or another in class. On the day the classroom was unrecognizable. All the double desks had been replaced with single tables. Any work that had been pinned up on the walls during the term was covered over and there was a person overseeing the exam whom I had never seen before. None of our regular teachers were allowed to be present. It was really quite intimidating.

The exam, conducted in total silence, again not something that I was used to, was split into several sections:

- Arithmetic
- Writing
- General Problem Solving

Failing the exam meant that I would go to Bridley Moor Secondary Modern School in the new school year. This would not have been a bad thing as this was where both Margaret and Jane Fowkes attended. Passing the exam meant that I would be offered a place at Redditch County High School, which was where Peter had gone having passed his 11+ three years earlier. It was a simple pass or fail. There was no account taken of course work nor of teachers' opinions or children's nerves on the day. Pass or fail, that was it.

I remember going home afterwards when both Mum and Dad said that as long as I had done my best, then no-one could ask any more of me. They said they didn't mind which school I went to as Peter was at the Grammar School and Martin had been at Bridley Moor.

It was well into the summer holidays before everyone got the results by letter from the Education Authority. I was playing with Michael James outside – the James family had moved into 117 Foxlydiate Crescent when the Fowkeses moved out. Michael was known as Pickle although I have no idea where this originated. Pickle's dad, who worked permanent night shifts, came outside and told him that he was to be going to Bridley Moor. I rushed indoors and saw that the postman had been. The letter was on the mat but neither Mum nor Dad were there – they were both working and wouldn't be home until later that day. I had to wait for what seemed like forever before Mum came home. She opened the letter and told me that I would be going to the Grammar School – I had passed the 11+. I was so pleased but at the same time I felt guilty because Pickle had failed. Looking back, to categorise someone of 11 years as a failure must have been an horrendous blow to their self-confidence.

Auntie Mabel had promised that, if I passed, then she would buy me a leather satchel. She kept her promise and, just before September 1965, I was indeed presented with a beautiful chestnut-coloured satchel.

One thing that springs to mind occurred just before I left Holyoakes Field. We were taken to the new school for a familiarisation day. I had only ever worn shorts to school before, but Mum decided that as I was now going to "big" school, she would buy me a pair of long trousers which I was allowed to wear on this day.

I felt really grown up as we were shown around the school until, that is, I was walking down some concrete steps towards the gym when I slipped and fell, tearing a hole in the knee of my brand-new trousers. I went home expecting the worst, but Mum took it all in her stride and sent the trousers to be "invisibly" mended.

My mum never ceased to amaze me, even in later life, with the strength she had, the love she was able to give and the way she held our family together, even when Dad was working away in Bristol. I should tell you about this chapter in our lives.

In 1964 Mum and Dad were talking about going to live in Weston-super-Mare. We had enjoyed several good holidays there and living by the seaside was an attractive prospect.

School summer holidays 1964 – me (left) proudly trying on my new uniform (complete with invisibly-mended trousers) with the satchel that Auntie Mabel had bought for me – and Peter looking really cool! Taken in the back garden of 115.

Dad managed to get an interview in Bristol with British Aircraft Corporation (BAC), later to become British Aerospace and now part of BAE Systems. The Conservative Government of the time had commissioned the building of a new, then Top Secret, fighter/bomber codenamed TSR2 and BAC had won the contract.

Dad was an experienced aircraft sheet metal worker and fitter – he had served in the Royal Navy Fleet Air Arm during World War II on the "Sunderland" flying boats, used for Atlantic patrols, and Bristol was only a short distance from Weston. Everything seemed to be slotting into place.

Dad, Mum and I travelled down to Bristol in Uncle Eric's grey A35 van where Dad was interviewed and shown around the factory. I sat in the front between Uncle Eric and Mum, no seat belts at that time of course. Dad was trying to make himself comfortable on cushions in the back of the van. The van was not fitted with modern flashing indicators – it had orange trafficator arms which slid out from each side, and which were operated by a round switch on the dashboard. I was allowed to operate these at appropriate times although once or twice there was a little panic as Uncle Eric turned one way not realising that I had turned the trafficator to point the other way!

A few days later, Dad was offered the job and accepted. It was going to take some time to arrange physically moving to a new house and so Dad went into lodgings with a Mr. and Mrs Dyer in Patchway, Filton – only a bus ride away from the factory.

Dad would travel to Bristol on Sunday nights then come home the following Friday. This went on for several months. On Wednesday or Thursday every week Mum and I would walk up to the post office to the telephone box. At 7 o'clock on the dot Dad would ring her. Woe betide anyone who might have already been using the telephone as the time approached!

Dad wrote letters to me and Peter while he was away and would include football programmes from Bristol City and Bristol Rovers matches he had been to see. I missed him so much and it was wonderful to see an envelope bearing Dad's handwriting dropping through the letterbox for me. A real handwritten letter, unlike the impersonal emails and texts of today.

However, in October that year things began to fall apart. Dad had been offered a house in Weston, but a General Election had been called which saw a

Labour Government elected to Downing Street by a tiny majority. The reader might think that there was no connection between us moving to Bristol and Harold Wilson being asked by The Queen to form a government. Although both Mum and Dad had been staunch Labour supporters all their lives this result was to cost us dearly and change our lives once more.

I mentioned that the Conservative Government had commissioned the TSR2. One of the first actions that Prime Minister Wilson took was to cancel this contract. The TSR2 was never to be. No TSR2 meant no job for Dad. No job for Dad meant no move to Weston for us. And so it was that Dad came back to Redditch where we continued to live. Such is fate – and Governments!

I don't remember exactly when but another move that had been planned by Mum and Dad was an even bigger one. Emigration to Australia. The Aussie Government were looking for people with Dad's skills to work in the Antipodes and so all the paperwork was completed, and it was agreed by the Australian employment and immigration authorities that we would go. This was known as the £10 voyage because that is all that the voyage by ship would cost for each person. The travel tickets having been booked, it was Mum this time who put a halt to this move. She decided that she couldn't leave her Mum and Dad, my Granny and Grandad. The whole thing was called off. I remained a Pommie for ever more!

I go back three years now. In 1961 Gyp came along. I am not sure of the reasons as to how we came to have a dog – it might have been something to do with Mum's health – but one evening Dad came home with this tiny black bundle. I was 7 years old at this time and we had Gyp until she passed away when I was 17. Looking back as a child, I can hardly remember *not* having her. She was a black mongrel with more than a few breeds contained somewhere in her DNA. We grew up together, we explored the countryside and played games. We were the best of buddies. I was heartbroken when she died.

There are so many stories about Gyp, and I will recall some of them here.

For whatever reason, Gyp hated the dustmen. Whenever they came, she would go wild. It wasn't helped because I used to wind her up. I would hear them arrive and I would say "Here come the……… DUSTMEN!" She very quickly came to know this phrase and considered it perfectly acceptable to try and break her way through the door. The word "chocolate" came to have the same effect. If I was to lie next to her and say, "Shall we have some…" before I even got to the word chocolate she was bouncing up and down and barking. Of course, at that time we didn't realise that to our canine friends chocolate is quite toxic.

Gyp used to hate fireworks. Late October into November was a nightmare for her. She would tremble with fright if she heard them and would crawl under the stove in the kitchen. There was no way that she would be coming out until all evidence of fireworks had disappeared. On bonfire night, we would always get some tranquillisers from the vet for Gyp so she would quite happily sleep through all of the bangs and flashes.

At this time there seemed to be an outbreak of pushing lit bangers through people's letterboxes by older kids who thought this would be very funny. Pickle's Dad came up with a contraption that could be affixed onto the inside of the door for the evening and night to make such actions impossible.

Gyp had her own old armchair which sat in the corner of the kitchen. This was her space. If she was in trouble for any reason we would say "GET IN YOUR CHAIR!" and she would slink off into it, ears back, tail down.

Spillers Shapes biscuits were a treat for Gyp. They came in a variety of shapes and colours but, for some reason, she never ate black ones. Any of the others were fine, but not the black ones. Subconsciously, I wonder if this maybe had any bearing on my phobia of eating green sweets!

During school holidays Gyp and I would play and walk for miles. Bentley watersplash was a favourite place to go. This was about a mile and a half away from home through the countryside of Webheath. It was located in a tiny country lane with a ford that ran across the road together with a concrete raised area where one could walk, or ride bicycles, past it rather than through it. Often, Pickle would come along with his dog, Dougal. Now, *there* was a crazy animal. It would eat absolutely anything – food, clothes, paper, he even ate the electric plug off their washing machine on one occasion.

Gyp was about 3 years old when it was discovered that she was pregnant. She had a habit of slipping her collar or escaping from the garden. The inevitable had clearly happened and some weeks later she presented us with ten tiny puppies.

Now the next part I wasn't aware of until I read Dad's memoirs only a few years ago. The vet told Mum and Dad that Gyp would not be able to cope with

Bentley Watersplash – Upper Bentley, Redditch.

mothering and feeding ten pups and so, according to what Mum and Dad told me at the time and what I believed for nearly 40 years, we were asked to choose three to keep and the vet would take the remaining seven and find homes for them. I took this at face value and had no reason to think otherwise. When the seven had gone Gyp spent days hunting around the house for them.

It was so sad to see this and upset everyone greatly. She knew that there were more than three puppies, and it was a couple of weeks before she gave up on them. When, years later, I read Dad's book *This is How it Was*, I couldn't believe what I was reading. It seems that Dad had actually chosen the three pups to keep and, in reality, had taken the remaining seven up the top of the garden, drowned them in a bucket of water, and buried them.

At the time, reading this upset and angered me so much. For so many years I had believed what I had been told. I remember speaking to Mum about it and she thought that I had been told years before. In fairness to Dad, the act of carrying out this task, Mum said, upset and affected him dreadfully, as he documents in his book.

But, if you can read this, Dad, I understand and forgive you.

Gyp.

On another occasion Gyp, who was always a very inquisitive beast, explored one place too many and disturbed a wasp nest. Suddenly, she was engulfed by what seem like hundreds of wasps. I have never heard a dog squeal so much as she was stung time and time again. That was another trip to the vet, and she was lucky to recover, but recover she did.

Dad always loved football, and this rubbed off not so much on Martin but certainly on me and Peter. I have already spoken about going to the Valley Stadium to watch Redditch Town play. Dad had played a great deal of football in his younger days including playing for Redditch. It would be true to say that, had it not been for the outbreak of war in 1939 when he was just 19 years old, it is likely that he would have played professionally. Certainly, Sheffield United were looking to sign him but the war took its toll and, six years later when the world returned to a state of peace, his chance had gone. He did, however, play for St Mirren when he was stationed in Scotland during the war years.

My interest in football really blossomed in 1962 when World Cup matches were shown live from Chile on TV. In 1963 I recall getting ready in front of the TV to watch the FA Cup Final between Manchester United and Leicester City at Wembley Stadium. United were close to relegation from the topflight that season but Leicester was well placed in the top half of the table so were therefore odds-on favourites to win. I told Dad that I thought United would win; he said Leicester. So, I had a bet with him. I bet him two shillings (the cost of nearly 60 cigarettes in those days) that United would win. Dad mowed the lawns while the match was being played and I pulled the curtain in the front room to get as good a picture as possible on a pretty awful television.

Well, United, with Denis Law and Bobby Charlton leading the attack, only went and won 3-1 against all the odds. Dad kept his side of the bargain and coughed up two shillings which was probably 6 weeks' worth of pocket money for me. It's a good job that United did win because goodness knows from where I would have found two shillings to give to Dad. That would probably have *cost* me six weeks of pocket money!

Chapter Four

Redditch Carnival

REDDITCH CARNIVAL was an incredibly popular event that was always held in the town centre on the same early September day as the "Last Night of the Proms" was shown in the evening on TV. Thousands of people would go, and extra buses would be put on to get people there. There were four buses that went from the Batchley top shops into town – R1, R2, R21 and R22 – and the queue waiting to get on would be 40 or 50 people long. It was often easier and quicker to walk into town.

There were two fun fairs that set up in the town. One was in Church Green West on both sides of the road. The other was behind the Royal Hotel in Market Place. They were both massive and had all the usual sorts of attractions: dodgem cars, waltzers, ducks in water, air rifles, slot machines – you name it, they had it. However, the main objective for us on arriving in town was always to find a place from where we could watch the procession of floats. These were amazingly inventive and a glorious sight as they filed past. The procession consisted of anything up to 60 or 70 floats with various brass, drum, or pipe bands in between. The route varied slightly each year and the programme, issued a couple of weeks beforehand, would show the route for that day. The crowds on the pavement would be 10 or 12 deep in places so we had to get there as early as possible. It didn't matter if it rained, we would either have an umbrella or we would just get wet. We knew when the procession was getting close because there would be a police car at the front with its blue lights flashing. The making and preparing of floats would have been going on for several weeks beforehand and there were prizes for the best. Most were built on the back of flatbed lorries or on trailers hauled by tractors. The sights were quite magnificent, and we were always on the lookout for people that we knew. The Carnival Queen and her attendants would have a float all of their own. The Queen would be seated on a huge throne, and we would all shout and wave at her.

Mum and Dad would give us a handful of pennies, half-pennies (or ha'pennies as they were known) and, in the late 1950s, farthings.

Note – For those reading this who were not around before coin decimalisation in 1971:

- *A penny was worth 0.4 pence of today*
- *A ha'penny was worth 0.2 pence of today*
- *A farthing was worth 0.1 pence of today*
- *There were 12 pennies in a shilling – 5 pence today*
- *Two shillings made a florin – 10 pence today*
- *Two shillings and sixpence made a half-crown – 12 and a half pence today*
- *There were 240 pennies in a pound*
- *There were 20 shillings in a pound*
- *Banknotes came in denominations of 10 shillings, £1, £5 and, later, £10*
- *Pounds were shown as today – £, shillings as a small s and pennies as a small d, so, one pound, ten shillings and sixpence would be written £1-10s-6d. Two shillings and thruppence would be written as 2/3*

To put this in context, in the late 1950s:

- *The average weekly wage was £9 5s*
- *An average 3-bedroom house with a large garden cost £2064*
- *A gallon of petrol cost 4s 6d. Given that there are roughly 5 litres in a gallon this works out as 11 old pennies per litre or the equivalent today of 4 and a half pence per litre.*
- *20 cigarettes cost the equivalent of five and a half new pence.*
- *For £1 you could have bought 15 pints of beer!*

Redditch Carnival procession circa 1969, photo courtesy of Allelys.

Anyway, I digress. So we, usually me and Peter, had a pocketful of coins and the object was to throw the coins onto the floats of your choice. The people on them would collect them up (I must admit to seeing several ending up with cuts on their faces from flying coins) and put them into buckets. Money so collected would later be donated to a whole raft of charities.

The procession would travel very slowly and seemed to last forever until, that is, a second police car arrived at the rear and you knew then that that was the end. Actually, not quite the end… I said that we, in the same way as hundreds of other people, would throw coins onto the floats. Of course, not all coins made it to the float and so, once the procession had gone, there were throngs of young kids scouring the roads and footpaths for stray, wayward coins. It is surprising how much we were always able to find that gave us more money to spend on the fun fair.

Carnival Day was a wonderful affair, and it would be somewhere approaching 7 o'clock before Mum and Dad decided that it was time to go home. However, there would still be time for one of the day's highlights – hotdogs with onions! Now, most of the carnival hotdog stalls provided, more or less, a bread roll filled with a frankfurter sausage that had been heated up in water topped with hot tinned onions. The stall by the library, though, in Church Green West on the corner by Church Road had real sausages and onions which they fried as you watched so this was always where we headed. I can smell and taste them as I write!

Home we would go on the bus carrying with us the various things that we had won on the fair. These amounted to animals made from chalk which, when they were broken a couple of weeks later were perfect for marking out the pavement for hopscotch, and a variety of other cheap prizes. There was only one rule – we were never allowed to choose a goldfish as a prize!

As an aside, the same rule applied when the rag and bone man periodically came through the Crescent with his horse and cart. In exchange for old clothes he would have toys and games on board to give to us, and goldfish! We were never destined to have a goldfish.

Once home and very tired, Mum would prepare supper, usually sandwiches, crisps and pickles, and we would be allowed to stay up and watch Sir Malcolm Sargent conducting the orchestra on the TV during the *Last Night of the Proms,* which always fell on the same date as the carnival. It is likely that I would have fallen asleep long before *Jerusalem, Land of Hope and Glory* and the *Sailor's Hornpipe* were performed.

I mentioned that we travelled by bus to and from the carnival. This reminds me vividly of the bus journey up Bates Hill, a really, *really,* steep hill. I said earlier that I would tell you about this. Now buses, especially double decker buses, were renowned for struggling to get up normal hills let alone Bates Hill. There are two things I recall vividly. Firstly, at the bottom of Bates Hill there was a railway bridge and quite a low railway bridge at that. When double decker buses, before my time, were first routed to go underneath this bridge they tended to scrape the top of it – not good. On one occasion, a bus managed to get stuck fast. Air had to be let out from the tyres before there was enough clearance for the bus to drive on. This led to the Redditch Urban District Council digging out some of the road underneath the bridge so that buses could pass through without any damage being caused to the bridge, the bus, or passengers. You can imagine how terrifying it was, then, to be travelling in the seat at the front of the top deck as you approached the bridge. Every single time it looked to all and sundry as though the top of the bus would be ripped away by the top of the bridge. Right at the last second the bus would dip down where the road had been lowered (by which time I was normally prone on the floor!) and the bus would pass through.

As if that wasn't enough, the bus then had to negotiate Bates Hill itself to reach town. Well, the driver would drop down into third gear, then second

Redditch Bus Station mid-1960s. I would catch the R1, R2, R21 or R22 from the corrugated iron shelter on the right.

and even into first, especially if the bus was fully loaded, before it managed to crawl up the hill. This was even scarier if the driver missed a gear, and the bus might roll back slightly. I think my love of walking must have materialised around this time!

The bus station for what were nicknamed the Midland Red buses (the company was actually called the Birmingham and Midland Motor Omnibus Company Limited) was situated just off Market Place in Redditch. The turning was right next to a piece of waste ground upon which had previously stood the Regal cinema where Granny used to work. To call it a bus station is something of a misnomer, especially when one compares it to the grand structures of today. Buses would offload passengers when they drove in, then circle the station before parking up beside a number of corrugated iron stands ready for the next load of passengers to board.

Buses, whether single or double decker, always had a crew of two. The driver, who did just that, plus a conductor or conductress bearing a manual ticket machine from a leather strap around their necks and who would be responsible for walking up and down the bus collecting fares and issuing tickets. Once paid, a handle would be turned on the machine and a ticket

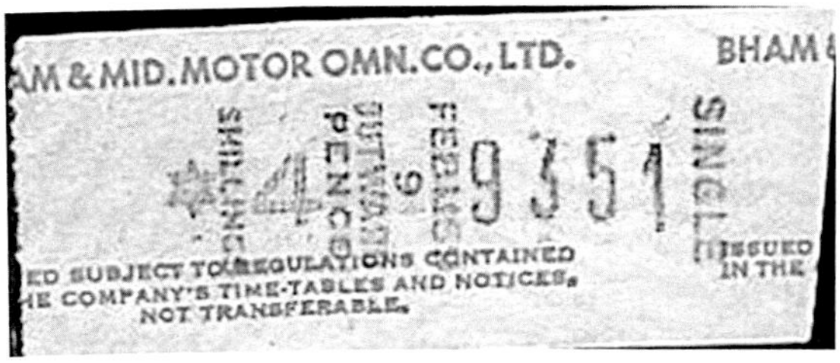

A "Midland Red" bus ticket – mid 1960s.

produced. There was not a great deal that one could do with the ticket so, invariably, one would end up folding it, rolling it, trying to make a miniature paper plane out of it – which was all very well unless the Inspector got on and demanded to see you ticket. No ticket – no travel in most cases. For anyone who has watched the TV comedy *On the Buses*, Blakey is probably as close as you can get to a real bus inspector! It was often a case of trying to reshape the ticket into a form good enough for the inspector to read. It was always a bit of a panic when the inspector boarded.

Smoking was allowed on double decker buses but only upstairs. As children we loved to travel on the top deck, but it was often the case that we were sat in the middle of this bluey/grey haze. I also remember that there was always a sign on the platform by the door which read "Do not alight until the bus has stopped." For years and years, I was convinced that this meant not lighting a cigarette or pipe while the bus was moving. Of course, people did, and I could never understand why the conductor did nothing about it! I was somewhat older before I realised the true meaning.

If we had to catch a bus from home the nearest bus-stop was about 100 yards from our house. The bus had to come past the house to get to the top shops where it turned around and came back on the return leg. Once the bus had gone past our front door we knew that we had about 10 minutes to get ourselves ready and reach the bus-stop before the bus came back. We usually made it, but I can remember some occasions when our judgement failed, and the bus went sailing past us, despite us waving to try and stop it.

There were other fairs and carnivals that happened during the year. The Cherry Wake was a largish fair that took place at Headless Cross on waste ground on the junction of Birchfield Road and Plymouth Road. This was always in late spring when the cherry blossom had dropped off the trees, hence the name. On the topic of cherry trees, at the bottom of The Patch, there were two enormous flowering Japanese cherry trees. Both must have been in excess of fifty feet tall. Each spring, their display of cherry blossom was extraordinary and breathtaking. Once the blossom dropped off the branches, The Patch took on the appearance of being covered in pink and white snow.

There was also Crabbs Cross carnival which occurred each summer. A smaller event than Redditch but good to visit, nonetheless. It had its own procession and I remember my cousin June, daughter of Auntie Lil and my

Mum's twin brother, Uncle Jack, dressed up as Little Bo Peep for one of the floats one year. This was the year that Auntie Lil was pregnant with her second daughter, Ann.

Crabbs Cross carnival circa 1962. Photo taken at the junction of Evesham Road and Jubilee Avenue. L to R Granny Thornton, Grandad Thornton, Mum, Peter, my cousin June (daughter of Auntie Lil and Uncle Jack) as Bo Peep, Auntie Lil (pregnant with Ann), me and Mum's twin, Uncle Jack.

Me, June and Peter.

Chapter Five

The Winter of 1962/1963

I HAD just had my ninth birthday when Christmas 1962 arrived. As children (and still as adults) we always dreamed of there being a white Christmas. Bing Crosby sings about it, Christmas cards often show snow on the ground, Dickens *A Christmas Carol* is set in a snowy Yuletide. The reality is, however, that it rarely occurs, at least not at Christmas itself. There is an old saying though; be careful what you wish for because you might just get it.

On Christmas Day that year there was no snow, so we were all a little disappointed. It was very windy, though, and bitterly cold. We, as always, had a lovely Christmas Day. I think this was the year that I was given my Scalextric set so much of the day would have been spent playing with that. At the end of what was probably a very tiring day all round, off we went to bed.

Snow began to fall on Boxing Day, very heavily, but no-one could have foreseen just how bad it would get. It turned out to be one of the coldest winters on record with lakes, rivers and even the sea freezing over. In Herne Bay, Kent, the sea froze over for a distance of a mile from the shore and four miles out to sea from Dunkirk in northern France. Although there was a brief respite, a couple of days later the snow returned with a vengeance. Over New Year, blizzards swept across the country causing several feet of snow in places and drifts up to twenty feet. This continued until the beginning of January and then, with temperatures as low as -20°c during the day, the country froze solid. Freezing fog, for days and nights on end, added to the misery and chaos. Cars were able to drive across the River Thames in Oxford and near London!

At Foxlydiate I remember seeing icicles, hanging from gutters, which were over three feet long and as thick as a drainpipe. Residual ice perpetually formed on the inside of our windows. Dad spent hours in his old Naval duffle coat, clearing snow and breaking ice. There was very little, if any, vehicular movement in or through the town. Remarkably, however, life went on although activities such as shopping took much longer and required careful planning. Because the coal merchants were unable to deliver, Mum and I had to buy coal for the fire from the hardware store at the bottom shops by Batchley pond. We dragged it back home on an old sledge. Although there were a couple of days when they were closed, we went to school every day. We walked through frozen snow which was anything from 6 inches to a foot and a half deep, in short trousers and long socks to get to Holyoakes Field school. No buses ran properly for what seemed like weeks.

We sat in the classrooms with our coats and scarves on. The free one-third of a pint milk that we had during the mid-morning break was solid in its bottle with the silver foil cap having been pushed off due to the milk expanding and had to be thawed using the meagre heat emitted from the ancient radiators.

Lukewarm milk – yuk!

Frozen milk on the doorstep was a common sight.

Instead of leaving school at four o'clock we were allowed to leave at half past three so at least some of the walk home could be made during full daylight.

Dad would use the Foxlydiate Hotel, known locally as The Fox, as his local pub. This meant walking up the ash path and crossing Birchfield Road to get from one side to the pub side.

Ordinarily, Birchfield Road at this point had a five feet high hedge next to the pavement. The depth of drifting snow meant, however, that one could not see where the hedge finished and the path and road began. In fact, for many weeks, one could not see the hedge at all.

Any notion of playing outdoor sport was completely out of the question. The football FA Cup third round lasted a total of 66 days and featured no fewer than 261 match postponements. Matches should have been played on 5th January 1963. The last match of the third round eventually took place on 6th March! Sixteen of the thirty-two ties were called off ten times or more. Birmingham City's tie with Bury was the worst hit, stretching through 14 postponements, an abandonment and a replay.

I recall a steam train in the tunnel by Redditch Station becoming stuck because of frozen snowdrifts. It remained so for over two weeks. The weather took a heavy toll on elderly and infirm people. Smallwood Hospital was full to bursting and, as with many places in the UK during this time, the mortality rate rose significantly. The accident rate rocketed too, both for pedestrians and vehicles. The most tragic, though, involved a young lad, probably aged about 13, who lived on the Batchley.

Batchley pond had frozen over completely to the point whereby one could fairly safely walk over it. Indeed, I went playing on the frozen surface many times during the big freeze myself without any issues.

In the middle of the pond was a small island from which grew a few trees and bushes. The boy walked on the ice over to the island and, fatefully, decided to climb one of the trees. I wasn't there but it seems that he lost his handhold, slipped and fell, head-first, onto the ice. The injuries he suffered were, alas, too severe for him to stand any chance of survival. The passing of the youngster stuck in my mind and I never again went walking on the frozen wastes of Batchley pond.

It was not until mid-March that winter finally loosened its icy grip in the Midlands but even on Easter day on 14th April there was still a good deal of snow on the ground where drifts had been at their deepest. It was truly a marvel to see signs of green grass once more. We had got so used to looking out of the window onto a scene of white and grey.

It was a long time before I ever wished for a white Christmas again and, even today, people still talk about that winter especially those who, like me, experienced it, lived through it and came out the other side.

Chapter Six

Autumns

THE ONSET of Autumn meant a number of things. Firstly, as the days grew shorter and the nights drew in, Mum and Dad used to buy me and Peter a torch each. This happened every year, mainly because torches were never used in the Spring and Summer which meant that batteries leaked – because we failed to remove them – and corroded all over the inside. Come the Autumn, of course they would not work. With shiny new torches, however, we could go out into the Crescent after dark, until about 7 o'clock, to play with our friends. One year I was lucky enough to be bought a torch which could show three different lights: white, red or green. By shining the light up into my face from below my chin I could be a devil, a genie, a ghost or whatever. I loved that torch, but I expect it went the same way as all the other torches.

The second thing about Autumn was that this was the time for chestnutting! At the far end of Pitcheroak Wood, just before reaching Red Lane (where the Bromsgrove Highway bridge now crosses the road) there were three massive sweet chestnut trees, and this was where the best and biggest chestnuts were to be found. Me, Peter and Dad would spend a Saturday or Sunday afternoon kicking through a golden carpet of leaves which had already fallen, looking for the chestnut treasures that lay beneath. However, the cherries on the cake were those that remained on the tree, twenty or thirty feet up. We would have to find a branch or small log, which was not too heavy to throw up at the chestnuts but weighty enough to dislodge them. Once the husks were on the floor, we would roll them underfoot to release the nuts inside. We would take pocketfuls of them back home which we would either eat raw, although it took an age to get the white inner pithy skin off, or we would roast them by placing them on the grate of the open fire making sure we pricked them first to avoid them exploding as the pressure built up inside. Sometimes we forgot with inevitable results. Roast chestnuts on a cold and dark autumn evening – nothing better. We always said we would keep a batch for Christmas, but they were always eaten well before then.

The very best thing about Autumn was Bonfire Night. In the 1950s and 60s, it was usual to build the biggest bonfire you could in your back garden. The gardens in the Crescent were all wide and long so there was always plenty of room to build quite a tall, substantial bonfire. We would start collecting newspapers, wood, orange boxes from local shops and anything else that would burn, several weeks before the event. We would keep all these combustibles in the garden, but we would never build the bonfire, or "bonny," until a day or so before the event. Then we would guard it through the evenings until 5th. The reason for not building and then guarding was that it was not unusual for bonfires to be set alight by other older children in the neighbourhood in the days leading up to 5th. This happened to us one year – I must have been 9 or 10. We were sitting in the dining room having our tea (we would

Not us, but a typical way we used to build bonfires in the 1950s and 60s.

call it dinner these days) when we realised that the night sky was no longer dark. Our bonny had been fired. We had a good idea as to who the culprits were – a family six or seven doors away – but we could never prove it, and, in any event, the bonfire was no more so there was nothing we could do. This was on the evening of 4th. Martin, who was about 16, and his friends all got together that night. Between them, over the next few hours, they built us a brand-new bonfire. That year we had the best bonfire ever.

The greatest times were had when the Fowkeses lived next door. We always had a joint bonfire party. One year we would provide the jacket potatoes that cooked in the embers of the fire and Mrs Fowkes would serve up hotdogs and fried onions. The next year would be the other way around.

There was a wire fence separating our back gardens but, no matter how many times Dad or Mr. Fowkes repaired it, it would always get broken and trodden down by us climbing over into Margaret and Jane's garden, or they into ours. We would extract the fireworks that we had amassed in the clothes cupboard over the preceding weeks and Dad would buy a couple of extra boxes as well. We would then plan in what order we would let them off. It was all very scientific! Maybe a couple of Roman Candles to start with, then rockets which would generally be launched from a milk bottle, maybe a Jumping Jack or two (which always frightened me because I imagined one jumping up and going down my wellie!). The Catherine Wheel usually provided something of a challenge. Dad would have to find somewhere for it to go then we would have to find a nail and a hammer to fix it whilst ensuring that it could spin freely. It sometimes didn't, but we didn't mind too much! One year the wheel started to speed round so fast that it disengaged itself from the wood and nail and flew through the air. No harm done though. The biggest decision to make was, which firework were we going to leave until last? Most boxes had that one special firework and that would be fiercely protected until the last moment. These were great nights at a time when it would have been really unusual to go to an organised display. I could look along the line of back gardens and probably see half a dozen bonnies alight. It was always a bit of an unannounced competition as to whose was the biggest and which one lasted the longest.

The following morning, if it wasn't a school day, my friends and I would scour the streets collecting up all of the spent fireworks and rockets that we could find. You could still smell the burnt cordite on them! I am not entirely sure why we collected them. I think they all just went into a box where they stayed for a couple of weeks before being thrown away.

Autumn time really was very special, but the transformation of Autumn into Winter meant two things – my birthday and CHRISTMAS!

Chapter Seven

A Good Holiday and a Good Christmas

IT IS something of a standing joke with Peter that, despite all our claims about being poor and having to slice the peas as well as the meat, in reality we were relatively well off and certainly more fortunate that many other families on the Batchley. I do remember, all joking aside, that on Sunday afternoons when we were watching television, Mum would bring in a single Mars bar and slice it up between the three boys. This never really worked – three boys and only two chocolate-covered ends! We took it in turns weekly as to which of us would have the "crusts" but of course we all swore blind that we had not had the "crust" the week before. Once we had possession of our chocolate Mum and Dad used to say that they were going for a "lie down" upstairs. I never thought twice about this at the time but when I was a little older it dawned on me what *really* used to go on upstairs. I realised that this was probably the only time of the week that they could have to themselves for such things.

Some things were normal with all families of that era – for instance, hand-me-downs. If there was a bit of wear left in clothes or shoes that no longer fitted either of my brothers then they used to come to me… and why not? The 1950s was a period of rebuilding and many still had the war mentality, "Make Do and Mend". I can remember Mum darning our socks or sewing patches onto coat elbows or trousers that had become worn. But, as I say, we were much better off than many. I remember one neighbour who, when he was about 12, never had any shoes. He had wellington boots to put on his feet and that was it. There is a photograph I recall seeing of the whole school where he attended, Bridley Moor Secondary Modern (now demolished) off Batchley Road, which would have been taken in the early 1960s when he was in the first or second year. He is seated, cross-legged, on the front row wearing his wellies.

I mentioned earlier that Mum used to work at home making springs. Other than when she was in hospital, I cannot recall a time when she did not work. And it was this additional income which, to a great extent, made it possible for us to have a week at the seaside every summer and a really good Christmas.

The summer holiday, for us, started around February when Dad would write to various seaside locations to obtain a free copy of their current brochure together with details of hotels and guest houses. That is another example that demonstrates we were not that badly off – we would always stay in a hotel wherever we went. Peter and I would wait for the first and second post deliveries every morning (yes, there really were two deliveries each day: one around 8am and the next just before lunch) in anticipation of the brochures arriving. If we were at school, we would have to wait until home time at 4pm to find out if there had been any post.

Weston-Super-Mare was the nearest seaside resort to us and so it was natural that most of our holidays would be spent there. The brochure, when it arrived, was in two parts. The first half of the book showed photographs of all the attractions and places to go and see. The second part listed all the hotels and guest houses in the town, detailing rooms, facilities, location and, of course, cost. Let me say that the second part was of no interest whatsoever to me and Peter. We poured over every page of photographs deciding and planning the best places going to go and what we were going to do. Mum and Dad would read through the details of copious numbers of hotels to find one that fitted the bill. For them, the hotel should have a bar. This would mean that when we were tucked up in bed, they could slip downstairs and have a drink. They would end up with a number of hotels marked with a cross in pencil as "possibilities." It would then be down to Dad to either ring the establishment which entailed a trip up the ash path to the Post Office telephone box with a handful of pennies (old pre-decimalisation pennies, that is) or, more likely, to write a series of letters, always enclosing a self-addressed and stamped envelope for the reply, asking about vacancies.

At the beginning of the 1960s, it cost 3d (or just over 1p) to post a letter in the UK. The GPO (General Post Office) increased the cost to 4d in 1965 but it wasn't until 1968 that it introduced a new two-tier system. One could still post a letter for 4d, but if you paid 5d it was more likely to be delivered the following day. This led to the eventual introduction of first and second-class postage.

The telephone box, as well as being a lifeline to Dad when he was working in Bristol, was in itself interesting. Firstly, it always worked and was never vandalised. In addition to the telephone itself there were two pushbuttons, one marked A and the other marked B. On lifting the handset, one would place two or three pennies into a slot. The number would then be dialled. If someone answered then, in order to be able to talk to them, it was necessary to push button A. This made the connection, and one could then talk away. When the money was used up the operator would come on the line with instructions to put more money in or, normally she, would terminate the call. If the number you were ringing just continued to ring out and no-one answered, then you would need to replace the handset and press button B. Your pennies were then returned to you. No answer machines in those days. If no-one was in then one would simply have to try again later, sometimes several times before successfully getting through.

The old A and B pushbutton telephone.

Back to the holidays. Eventually, the hotel was booked, and we had a week at the seaside to look forward to. This would usually be during the last week in July or the first in August which, at that time, was the working man's holiday when factories closed down. As holiday time came close Mum would again come into her own. She would make six lists – Dad, Mum, Martin, Peter, Anthony, Other (at least I came before Other!). Each of these lists would detail everything that we intended to take with us on our adventure and, as the day approached and suitcases packed, every item on the lists would be ticked off.

Getting to Weston-Super-Mare involved the successful completion of several journey stages:

- Home to Redditch Railway Station
- Train from Redditch Station to Barnt Green Station
- Train from Barnt Green Station to Bristol
- Train from Bristol to Weston-Super-Mare Station
- Walk or taxi from the station to the hotel

For Mum and Dad with three children, two suitcases plus all the paraphernalia that goes with a holiday, this was never an easy task. It always involved getting up "in the middle of the night," in reality about five o'clock in the morning, with me and Peter becoming increasingly hyper-excited, Martin not so much, so we were difficult to handle and this was the very beginning of what was always going to be an exceptionally long day! We used the same suitcases for many years. The largest had a cream and red small check pattern and came with fastener expanders. You could really pile things into this one. The other was Dad's demob suitcase, a rather drab, khaki affair that was given to him when he was demobilised from the Royal Fleet Air Arm in 1946.

The week before we went away, Dad would walk to Redditch Railway Station to buy the train tickets. Either me or Peter, or both of us, would go with him. This was about half an hour walk from home. In my mind, the purchasing of the tickets was the final confirmation that we were actually going! Also, we would go shopping with Mum (Dad rarely went shopping) to buy holiday "things." This almost always included a new pair of sandals, a pair of shorts and a tee-shirt or two.

Redditch Railway Station in the 1960s.

On the day we would take packed lunches, flasks with hot drinks and, if we were lucky, a bar of chocolate. We all had to carry something although I was something of a whinger who used to whine and protest against this. It did me absolutely no good though and I survived, normally with the threat of "if you don't carry your bag you won't be going to ... *whatever was chosen by Mum or Dad to have the maximum impact...* in Weston." It always worked.

Going off on a bit of a tangent, I can remember certain phrases that, particularly Mum, used. I am sure that readers of a certain age will recognise them:

- *"If the wind changes your face will stick like that"* – It never did.
- *"Put clean pants/socks on in case you have an accident"* – If I had an accident then the last things that Mum or Dad would worry about were clean pants or socks.
- *"Now be a good boy and be nice to your cousin"* – Forced niceness to someone you don't like is much worse than being openly hostile!
- *"If you don't eat your dinner you will have it for your breakfast tomorrow"* – I never did.

- *"Because I said so!"* – Used only when all other arguments had been exhausted and failed!
- *"Stop crying before I give you something to cry about"* – Luckily, I was very rarely smacked although that failed to prevent the perception that it might happen, so I would stop crying!
- *"If you say something like that again I'll wash your mouth out with soap"* – They never did, but, just in case, whatever I had said would not be repeated!
- *"Just wait until your Dad comes home"* – I heard this a few times and, thinking back, I feel sorry for Dad walking through the door after a hard day at work and not having a clue what was going on!
- And one very quickly learned that if you wanted something and you were told *"We'll see,"* then that meant No. It was a phrase used purely to buy time and prevent tears rather than just saying No from the outset!

Returning to the holidays, if we were lucky with the weather then most of our days would be spent on the beach. We would buy, or be bought, buckets, spades and packets of world flags on little sticks which we would place at the top of our sandcastle towers. If the weather was inclement, or the tide was in, then we would do something else. A morning or afternoon on a putting green was a great favourite and we would have family competitions. I seem to remember that, even in those days, Peter used to cheat – or at least try to! This might explain where I get it from – sibling influence. You see, NOT MY FAULT!

Being a specialist in metal working, Dad decided one year that he would make our spades. He did a great job and even etched our initials into each one so there would be no argument as to which belonged to whom. This was all very well but we very soon became aware that the spades were made from solid steel, and they were incredibly heavy, unlike the commercial ones one could buy on the sea front which were made of light wood and tin. Nonetheless, we persevered!

Another wonderful part of our week's holiday was that we were allowed to stay up late. After our evening meal we would go to the promenade to see all the illuminations that seemed to go on forever. Sometimes, our dinner would be fish and chips out of the paper, walking down the street – yummy!

We did have one or two minor disasters. One of the worst was when Peter was sunbathing and fell asleep in the sun. The back of his legs burned badly and turned a bright salmon pink. He was in agony for the next couple of days. This meant finding a local chemist to buy bottles of calamine lotion which Mum would liberally apply to the accompaniment of Peter's howling. Only having shorts, he walked around with these huge white patches of dried lotion all over his legs looking more like a piebald pony!

As the years passed and we became slightly more affluent, our one week at the seaside turned into two and we would go further afield. Morecambe, Blackpool, Lytham St Annes and elsewhere all benefitted from an Aston presence.

We went to Lytham St Annes two or three times. Once was in 1964. I remember the year because Mum, Dad, Peter and I all went into Blackpool on a tram one evening. Me and Peter were allowed to go to the cinema to watch The Beatles in their first movie, made in black and white, *A Hard Day's Night*. Afterwards, Mum and Dad met us, and we all ate fish and chips out of brown paper bags.

Another time was in 1967 during the so-called Summer of Love and the height of flower-power. Because we were that much older by this time, me and Peter were permitted to walk from Lytham into Blackpool on our own. Mum and Dad said they would meet us later by the pier. Walking to the town we decided that we would become "flower children" and raided people's gardens to pick whatever we could. By the time we got into Blackpool we were truly adorned with flowers which was highly amusing for us but not so for Mum and Dad when they met us a couple of hours later. I don't think either really felt the warmth of the flower movement that particular night! Music records blaring out from the entire length of the "Golden Mile," were all hits of the time: The Beatles, Rolling Stones, Scott McKenzie, The Seekers, The Tremeloes, The Monkees, The Hollies and many more.

Some of the places we went:

Gorlestone

Me hiding behind Mum with Martin in front.

Weston-super-Mare

The three of us boys with Dad.

The family travelling in style on Weston beach!

Me, Dad and Peter.

Morecambe

Peter, Dad (in a collar and tie!), Martin and me in the front.

Lytham St Annes

Peter, Mum, and me.

Once Bonfire Night was done and dusted then the things to look forward to were my birthday and a week later Christmas Day.

As much as Mum and Dad tried to make it special, my birthday on 17th December was always, and inevitably I suppose, wrapped up with Christmas. Sometimes I would have a combined birthday and Christmas present but would have to wait until Christmas Day to receive it. To be honest, because of all the excitement of Christmas this really didn't matter very much to me. Birthdays did mean, however, that I would receive an increase in pocket money each week and that my bedtime would be put back by half an hour.

There are two things that I remember vividly in the weeks leading to Yuletide. In Evesham Street there was a department store called Hollingtons. My Uncle Eric, the first husband of Pam (Mum's younger sister) worked there for a while. At the beginning of December, after the clocks had some weeks before been put back an hour, it would start to get dark around half past three. When I was about ten years old I would take the bus into town on a Saturday afternoon and make for Hollingtons. Throughout the rest of the year, the store specialised in merchandise such as furniture, carpets and kitchenware. However, every December they transformed the top floor into a huge toy shop which became an absolute magnet to children like me and I would spend what seemed like hours walking around the various toy sections looking at things like Meccano, big pedal cars, train sets and, one of the newest toys, Scalextric. I so badly wanted one of these racing sets. Toy car racing in our house meant me and Peter on our hands and knees on the front room mat (we didn't have a carpet then), each of us with a Dinky or Corgi diecast car in our hands, going around and around in circles using the edge of the mat as the racetrack. The nature of doing this meant that there could never be a fair race and, Peter being bigger and older than me, tended to be the perpetual winner; that is, if we didn't end up fighting because of the obvious disadvantages to me!

We used to have dozens of these diecast cars, all of which ended up broken, bent or destroyed. Of course, the first things to be thrown in the bin would be the boxes in which they came. After all, who would be interested in a Dinky car box?! Had we kept them all in pristine condition, with their boxes, they would be worth a small fortune today. But these were toys to be played with, not the collection items they have since become. Hindsight is a wonderful thing!

The second thing was all the secrecy surrounding the buying of family presents. I usually managed to save sufficient pocket money to allow me to (almost) afford what I wanted to buy the others. Mum and Dad would help me out if there was a little to be added. Peter, on the other hand (bless him!) was not so frugal or conscientious and always ended up wanting at this time of year. Me, being the caring, sharing, younger sibling that I was, flatly refused his requests for a loan! And so, it was the "Oliver" begging bowl for him to approach Mum and Dad. I am sure that suitable repayment arrangements were made.

I mentioned earlier about the three-coloured torch that I had one Autumn. When this no longer worked and was beyond any sort of repair I removed the batteries and hid my savings in the shell of the torch. I then hid the torch right at the back of the sideboard in the front room where I knew no-one would find it. Not being content with that I then bragged to everyone that I had plenty of money but that it was hidden where no-one would ever find it. I don't think that either Peter or Martin ever found it because no money ever went missing.

The downside of this was that just in front of, and effectively hiding, my torch were a set of amber-coloured Babycham glasses that Mum and Dad had been given years before as a wedding gift. One time when I was removing the torch to put more money in, I knocked one of them over and it smashed. I scooped up the broken glass and threw it in the dustbin outside, covering it with other rubbish and said nothing. It must have been over 20 years later that I confessed to Mum. She looked indignant then laughed. I think she might not have been so forgiving years previously!

Whenever I bought a present, I would give it to Mum and Dad to look after until the time came to wrap it. Mum's present I would give to Dad and vice-versa. One year I bought Mum a manicure set from Boots the Chemist. It had all the normal things: scissors, nail cutters, nail file plus other bits and pieces. It was contained in a zip-up light blue leatherette case. The cost was two shilling and sixpence or half a crown. The equivalent today is twelve and a half pence but the real value of my 2/6 given inflation over the years is something much more. I remember buying it at the counter and giving the shop assistant my money which I had been clutching in my hand for fear of losing it. The assistant smiled at me and remarked how warm the coins were from where I had been tightly holding them, and that my mum must be very important to me. How right she was.

Generally, Mum would work up until Christmas Eve whereas I had normally broken up from school about a week before then. I was left to my own devices and, I shamefully admit, I used to go hunting around the house to try and find those presents that Mum and Dad had bought for me. Always one step ahead of the game, Mum and Dad realised that I might be tempted so they were well and truly hidden, probably with the Fowkeses next door, and I never did find anything.

Just before Christmas Eve, Dad would get the decorations down from the loft and go to buy a tree. We invariably had a real tree, mainly because there was not an abundance of artificial trees on sale in the early days, and they were rather expensive. In later years, though, we ended up with an artificial one.

Tree baubles were made from very thin glass and so there were always some that were broken from the previous year, or that got broken by one of us boys as we placed them on the tree. These days one buys plastic covered wire bauble hooks to hang them on the tree. Mum used to have to get the sewing box out and make heaps of cotton loops that we could use.

The biggest challenge was always the Christmas tree lights. The set we had was several years old and, after having untangled them which seemed to take forever, we never expected them to work first time when we plugged them in. Surprise, surprise, we were never disappointed. Light strings in those days were such that if one bulb failed then the whole string failed. So, it was often my job to go around each bulb – and there could be fifty or more – to make sure, firstly, that none had come loose. If we were lucky, we found a loose one, tightened it up and the lights came on. If not then we had to try to find a way of discovering which bulb, or bulbs, had gone rogue and replace them. Now there were two ways of doing this; one, go to the shop and buy some new bulbs – we rarely did that because not many shops stocked spare tree bulbs and, if they did, they were often the wrong size – or two, Dad would take out his packet of cigarettes, remove the silver paper from inside, carefully separate the silver paper from the ordinary paper that was on the other side of it, then use small pieces of the silver paper to push into the, now void, bulb socket to make the connection. It always seemed to work but goodness knows how we never electrocuted ourselves or burned the house down!

Christmas Eve was special. This was the night when Father Christmas would come, when we wanted to go to bed early to make him arrive more quickly, but also when we wanted to stay up late so as not to miss anything that was happening in the house that night. We wanted to stay awake so that we might catch a glimpse of "him" – but we always fell asleep before "he" arrived and, when we awoke on Christmas morning, "he" had always been and gone.

I would typically awake that morning around 4 o'clock, as would Peter. We shared a bedroom when we were young, and I would whisper to him. "Has he been?" We would then forage around in the dark to discover whether the pillowcases we had left out were full or empty. If they were full we would call out to Mum and Dad, who had probably only been in bed for 3 or 4 hours, "can we open our presents yet?" The inevitable response was "No, go back to sleep. You can get up at seven!" With pillowcases full of, as yet unknown, goodies just waiting to be unwrapped, that was never going to happen. We would probably last until half past five before Mum and Dad reluctantly gave in. Christmas Day had begun.

So, what sort of wonders were contained in the pillowcase? Normally, some six or seven items. Always some chocolate, maybe some socks, an orange and then two or three smallish toys. I remember one year unwrapping a plastic soldier which was about six inches long. On his back was a thin polythene plastic parachute attached to him with thin cord. Very simply, one folded the parachute close to the soldier's body then threw the whole thing into the air – outdoors, of course. As it descended the parachute opened and the combatant would float gently to the ground. This was wonderful and I played for hours with this until one windy March day. I threw it as hard as I could up into the air, the parachute opened, then the wind caught it and it floated down the street, over the houses, into the distance and out of sight, never to be seen again. I searched for days trying to find it but never did. It could have gone miles. My military man definitely missed the drop zone! Once we had opened the presents, and most probably eaten the chocolate by this time, we put them all back into the pillowcase and descended on Mum and Dad in their bed to show them what Father Christmas had brought us – as if they didn't know! By the way, for us it was always Father Christmas, never Santa Claus.

Dad would get up and make him and Mum some tea. This was the only time of year (that I know of!) when Dad laced their tea with a drop of whisky.

Everyone would descend downstairs where, of course, the tree was by now surrounded by all sorts of brightly wrapped and oddly shaped gifts. Present giving and receiving was not allowed until after breakfast, so Mum would be off into the kitchen and before long the smell of frying bacon would waft through the house. I would look out of the window, bearing in mind that it was still dark outside, and could see that all those houses where there were young children had lights blazoned whereas all those with no children, or those who were much older, were still in darkness. While Mum was busy cooking breakfast, Dad would be setting the fire in the front room using the coal that had been saved in the weeks leading up to the big day. We had only two sources of heat – the coal fire and, in the kitchen, a paraffin heater. Before long, albeit after several failed attempts, there was something resembling a fire springing to life in the grate. Not very warm at first but before long the front room would be beautifully snug.

Meals were always eaten in the dining room, never in the front room. The family would all sit around the dining room table at more or less set times each day. Christmas Day was no exception and, before long, we were devouring bacon, eggs, tomatoes, mushrooms, fried bread and anything else that Mum had cooked – all on top of the chocolate we had already devoured a short time earlier upstairs. It was not unusual for one or more of us, normally me I must admit, to be complaining of a poorly tummy later in the morning.

Once breakfast was eaten and cleared away, and the turkey had been put into the oven, the time arrived for main present opening. Some families are quite organised about this – they hand out all the presents to those named on the gift tags and everyone opens their gifts together. Not the Astons! This was more of a disorganised scrum but great fun! To shrieks of "Look what I've got" and "Thank you, Mum and Dad" the discarded wrapping paper, so carefully applied only a few hours beforehand, would build up into a sizeable pile in the middle of the floor. A short time later, if it was dry outside, Dad would take all of the spent paper outside and burn it. Recycling was still many years away. In fact, if you mentioned the word "recycling" to anyone, it was assumed that you were going to cycle the same route that you had travelled before! There are a number of main presents that I well recall. One year, Mum and Dad decided that they would buy me a pedal car. Not having a great deal of money to spare, they bought me a second-hand car which Dad then painted to make it look like new. They decided that I should wake up on Christmas morning to see it in the bedroom. So, when we were fast asleep on Christmas Eve, Dad carried the car upstairs. I say carried – Mum often told me the story of that evening. They had had a party downstairs with some friends and neighbours. Apparently, both Mum and Dad had consumed far too much alcohol, Mum with her brandy and Babycham cocktail and Dad with the bitter beer poured from a Davenports Party Seven tin. As an aside, these tins never came with any sort of opening device and it was surprising how few people could find proper can openers when they needed them, the sort that you placed on the edge and lifted up to form a small triangular opening and the same on the opposite side – simple physics; air in one side, beer out of the other. No, it was never like that. It always seemed to be a job for a hammer and screwdriver or chisel. One hefty blow and the pressurised beer and froth went everywhere. This operation, for that reason, was generally carried out in the kitchen sink.

Back to my pedal car. Being somewhat less than sober, Dad started to carry the car upstairs but only got about halfway when he tripped and let go of the car which bounced all the way back to Mum at the foot of the staircase and into the wall, tearing some of the wallpaper and making a dent. By all accounts, Mum was less than impressed! Eventually the car was parked next to my bed. However, there was a second issue which did not manifest until Christmas morning when I awoke. Of course I saw the car so I was out of bed, into the driver's seat and pedalling all around the bedroom. What I did not know and Dad did not realise the consequences of was that, as part of him making my new toy look like new, he had used black boot polish to make the tyres gleam. They gleamed alright, but so did the copious number of black tramlines that I had left all over the linoleum floor... Dad was even less popular with Mum that Christmas morning! This was compounded by the fact that Dad had also fitted the car with a horn. I wasn't bothered that it was only about half past six in the morning. The horn was like manna from heaven for me but, unfortunately, not so much so for the rest of the household, nor for the Fowkeses next door, I fear!

The second present I remember was one I had been hankering after for months, if not years. A wrapped box was given to me. This was about 3ft (90cm) x 2ft (60cm) x 6in (15cm). I decided to open it very slowly, trying to

Me in my pedal car circa 1957.

remove each piece of Sellotape separately so as not to tear the paper (I still do that to this day. It drives my wife Kay nuts!). I am not often stuck for words but there, in front of me, was this wonderful Scalextric set – WOW! Not only that but others had bought me, as their presents, extra pieces of track and other accessories. Before long, with Dad's help of course, we were competing in Formula One racing on a huge figure of eight track which took up most of the available space on the front room floor. That was a real magical moment.

One year I was given a large toy mediaeval castle. This was made from reinforced cardboard and papier-maché. There was a base, four towers and a working drawbridge and portcullis. It was necessary to put the castle together to be able to play with it and the toy soldiers that came with it. The towers had long, sharp metal spikes protruding from the bottom with which you were able to affix each one to the main base. These days it would more likely by a Velcro fitting or similar. I had hours of fun with this castle, but I must have had an argument with Peter at some point because he recalls that I hit him with one of the towers, the metal spike digging deeply into his arm. I maintain to this day that this was an accident and that there was no intention for this to happen although Peter recalls it slightly differently and often dines out on the story by showing people his scar!

Then there is the story of Martin and Prince Charles' bicycle. It must have been around 1959/1960. At that time Dad worked for the Royal Enfield Company in Hewell Road, Redditch. They produced many things, including munitions during both World Wars, but later specialised in motorbikes and bicycles. That Christmas, Mum and Dad decided to buy Martin a bicycle. It made sense, because Dad would receive a hefty discount from the Enfield, as it was locally called. One of his colleagues told Dad that the company were displaying some bikes at an exhibition in Earls Court in London and that one of them had been fitted with many upgrades and extras so why didn't he

Royal Enfield where Dad worked – and the home of Prince Charles' bicycle. On the far left is Renown Springs where Mum worked for several years.

buy that. To cut a long story short, Dad agreed and paid the money from his savings account to the factory buying office. He was given a receipt and the bike was his. At this point the story takes a twist. Unbeknown to Dad, and everyone else below very senior management, it transpired that this particular bike, now in Dad's possession, had been promised to the Duke of Edinburgh as a present for Prince Charles, hence all the expensive extras being fitted. It was due to be presented to the Duke imminently during a visit to the Redditch factory.

Martin on Prince Charles' bicycle.

Mass panic ensued within the Board of Directors when they realised what had transpired and Dad was ordered to take the item back so that it could go with the Duke to Buckingham Palace. He was, apparently, threatened with all sorts of repercussions if he did not hand the bike over. Dad, being Dad, refused and when the pressure on him was raised even further, he produced the receipt he had been given at the buying office saying, "I paid for it, here is the receipt, the bike is mine and there is nothing you can do about it!" And there wasn't. The factory ended up, almost overnight, producing another bicycle of similar specification which was then presented to the Duke and which the Prince ended up riding. Martin enjoyed riding his "Royal" Royal Enfield bike for many years! 50 odd years later, Kay and I were fortunate enough to be presented to the Queen and Duke at St James' Palace in London. I was sorely tempted to relate the story to the Duke but decided against it in the end. I feel sure, however, that he would have seen the funny side.

Back to Christmas Day. Once us boys were thoroughly engrossed with our presents Mum spent the rest of the morning preparing Christmas dinner with Dad helping. Once the dinner was cooking and could be left it was then time for us to go next door to the Fowkeses or them to us (we used to alternate each year) for a celebratory drink. I would have to get dressed in what was akin to Sunday best for this traditional visit when sherry was normally the order of the day. Even I was permitted a very small glass of sherry. I felt very grown up! The Fowkeses were wonderful neighbours but more of them later.

The most splendid of meals was set on the table for us by Mum at 1 o'clock. Turkey, roast potatoes (cooked in goose fat) and all the trimmings was the order of the day. Mum and Dad were not great wine drinkers, a sign of the times in those days, but a bottle of white was normally produced which was enjoyed by all, or at least by Mum and Dad. The first Christmas wine I ever tasted (I was only ever allowed a sip) was a French Sauternes. It was incredibly sweet, much too sweet in fact, and I decided that I didn't like wine very much. I don't know if this was the reason but, to this day, I am not a great lover of white wine. Give me a good bottle of French red any day!

Christmas dinner was always a lavish affair and, some fifty or sixty years later, I can now fully understand why there is an overwhelming desire for adults to take a nap on Christmas afternoon!

Christmas afternoon was the time when the family came to visit. Granny and Grandad would arrive either with Auntie Pam and Uncle Eric or with Auntie Lil and Uncle Jack. They both had cars. Incidentally, a car was something we never had until I was well into my teens. Neither Mum nor Dad were very bothered about driving, nor could they have afforded a car. If we needed to go somewhere we always took the bus.

So, the rest of Christmas Day was spent at our house with the adults talking or sleeping and us children playing with our toys and presents or watching whatever was on the TV – a large wooden cabinet with a tiny screen upon which, if we were lucky, a reasonably watchable picture would be displayed. Of course, 3 o'clock was set aside for the Queen's Speech, something everyone fell silent for.

Most adults seemed to smoke in those far off days and it was nothing unusual to have to open the window during the afternoon and evening to let out some of the smoke. Goodness knows what this passive smoking, as it was later to become known, did for us younger ones. Dad smoked Woodbines or Players, Mum had Embassy tipped, Grandad always had a pipe on the go and I'm sure that the others smoked as well. Being Christmas there was also an abundance of cigars. Now that reminds me of a present we used to get that would be completely inappropriate and non-politically correct today. I used

Dad used to smoke these. There were no filter tips and they cost the equivalent of 3 pence in modern money.

to have a junior smokers kit which consisted of a liquorice pipe, some white sweet cigarettes, a few chocolate cigars and a chocolate ashtray together with chocolate matches. Again, I used to think I was really grown up because I could "smoke" along with all the adults!

Also, there never appeared to be any real concern about drinking and driving. I don't think Uncle Eric was able to drink alcohol because he suffered from diabetes, but others would have plenty of beer and spirits then think nothing of jumping in the car to drive home. That was just the way it was.

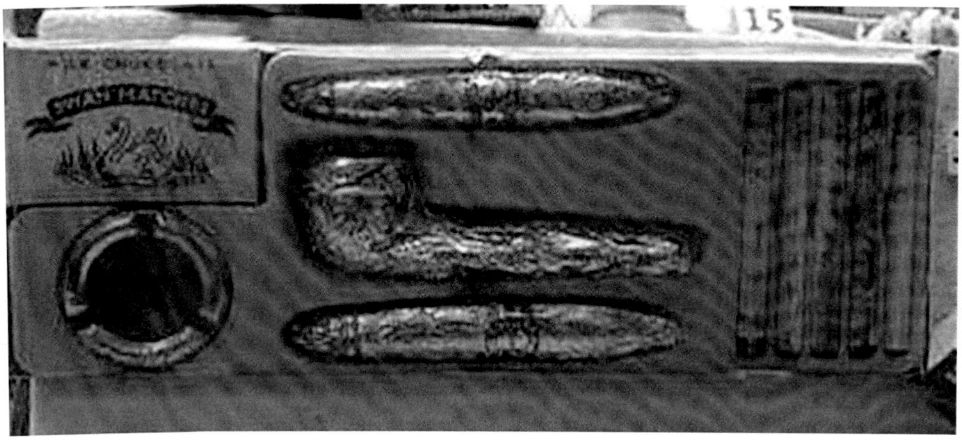

And this is what I would have "smoked"!

Bedtime on Christmas Day was always a disappointment, even though we might not have to go to bed until ten or 11 o'clock, because that meant that Christmas was over for another year. We would always know, however, that we had had a great time. And there was still Boxing Day to come with another special dinner, cold turkey and ham, cheeses, pickles, and the best thing of all… bubble and squeak… potatoes and vegetables from the previous day, all mixed and fried together. We would fight about who would have the lovely, slight burned pieces on their plate! Yes, there might have been a few tears or tummy aches along the way but when Peter and I joke about having "a good Christmas and a good holiday every year" that is exactly what we had, and I am enormously grateful to Mum and Dad for their efforts, the money they somehow managed to scrape together and for the sacrifices they made such that, at 68 years of age, I am able to remember these incredible times to the point where I feel compelled to write down my memories for the benefit of future generations.

Chapter Eight

Food and Drink 1950s and 1960s

WHEN I walk around Tesco or Sainsbury today and see the vast array of foodstuffs available it's difficult to imagine that, with much less choice, we actually ate very well as children. Indeed, albeit rationing was still around in part until the mid-50s, child obesity was relatively unknown and the amount of food we threw away was nothing compared to the seemingly mountains we dispose of today. A typical menu in the course of a week in the Aston household would have been:

Sunday:	*Breakfast*	Bacon and Egg or cereal
	Lunch	Roast joint with potatoes and vegetables
	Tea	Sandwiches, cake, crumpets in the winter (we called them pikelets – toasted with a toasting-fork in front of the open fire)
Monday:	*Breakfast*	Cereal and toast
	Lunch	Hot school dinner
	Tea	Pork or lamb chops with potatoes and vegetables
Tuesday:	*Breakfast*	Cereal and toast
	Lunch	Hot school dinner
	Tea	Sausages with mashed potatoes
Wednesday:	*Breakfast*	Cereal and toast
	Lunch	Hot school dinner
	Tea	Liver, onions and potatoes

Thursday:	*Breakfast*	Cereal and toast
	Lunch	Hot school dinner
	Tea	Meat pie with potatoes and vegetables
Friday:	*Breakfast*	Cereal and toast
	Lunch	Hot school dinner
	Tea	Fish and Chips
Saturday:	*Breakfast*	Bacon and Egg or cereal
	Lunch	Sandwiches or egg on toast
	Tea	Belly pork with potatoes and vegetables
	Supper	Cold meat rolls with pickled onions and crisps

All in all, we ate very well. Mum always ensured that there was wholesome food available for us and it would all have been homemade. Very little food was pre-packed and frozen food was unheard of.

Particularly during the 1950s, chicken was a luxury dish. Beef, pork and lamb were readily available and relatively cheap whereas we would only have chicken on occasions such as Easter (in addition, of course, to several chocolate Easter eggs!). The reasons for this probably surrounded the fact that all chickens were free range – not caged – and there was no mass processing.

Some other thought-provoking ditties:

- Curry was an unknown entity
- Olive oil was kept only in the medicine cabinet
- Herbs, other than mint, were used only to make rather dodgy medicines
- A takeaway was a mathematical problem
- A pizza was something to do with a leaning tower
- All crisps were plain, the only choice being whether to sprinkle the blue twist of salt on them or not
- All fizzy soft drinks were called pop
- Coke was something mixed with coal to make it last longer
- A Big Mac was what you wore when it rained
- Oil was for lubricating your bike and not cooking – lard was for cooking
- Tea was made in a teapot with real tea, not teabags

- Coffee was only drunk when there was no tea – and then it was liquid Camp which contained chicory and came in a bottle
- Figs and dates appeared only at Christmas, but no-one ever ate them
- Only Heinz made baked beans
- Leftovers went in the dog
- Filled potato skins – well, what would that have been all about?
- Nothing ever went off in the fridge because no-one had one
- No-one had heard of yoghurt
- A Chinese chippy was a foreign carpenter
- Healthy food was anything edible
- People who didn't peel potatoes were regarded as lazy unless they were cooked as jackets
- Indian restaurants were only found in India
- Christmas began at Christmas, not at the end of the summer
- Brunch was not a word, let alone a meal
- A tart was a fruit filled pastry, not a lady of horizontal pleasure
- The idea of "oven chips" made no sense at all
- Sugar was regarded as "white gold" and enjoyed good press
- Surprisingly, muesli was readily available; it was called cattle food
- Water came out of a tap – the suggestion of bottling it and charging for it would have made you a laughing stock. It always amuses today that water has been underground for millions of years but as soon as we put it in a bottle, a "Sell-by" date is stamped on the label. Most curious!

I invite any people reading this and who were born after 1970 to compare this list with the food that adorns the shelves and is thrown at us today from TV adverts and computer screens. Do you think you would have survived back then!?

And what were school dinners like? Well, whether one ate much of the food served up was more down to hunger than one's taste. My favourites were beef stew (if you were lucky, you would sometimes find meat in amongst the fat!) which we used to call hogwash. It was hot, thick and very tasty. It was guaranteed to stick to your stomach lining and keep hunger away until tea-time at home. Puddings could be delicious or awful. Ginger cake or steam pudding with lashing of hot (somewhat lumpy!) custard – sometimes *pink* custard – was the business. As was rice pudding. Tapioca, or frog spawn as we called it, I used to hate. Many loved it, but I just couldn't get the image of tadpoles out of my mind!

Any leftovers were, in those days, simply put into a large, lidded metal bin outside which would be collected by local farmers at some point and used as pig swill feed. No-one gave any thought to the future and how this might be identified as contributing to outbreaks of swine vesicular, and other, diseases in later years.

Mum used to go shopping into town on a Saturday morning. She would take two or three shopping bags. One would be the potato bag. Mum would buy her vegetables at the market then they would be put loose into the potato bag – potatoes first followed by carrots, then cabbage and cauliflower and finally any smaller pieces such as apples. Groceries would be bought from the only shop in Redditch that could be loosely termed as a supermarket. This was George Mason's in Evesham Street.

We went through a period when we would have shopping delivered. Batty's was a grocery shop located in Hewell Road opposite the junction with Batchley Road and next to A. Poole and Sons (which, remarkably, is still there). Mum would write what she wanted in a notebook, an order book effectively, which she would drop in Batty's. The shop would box everything up then deliver it a few days later. Not that different a process to Tesco on-line home delivery these days, I suppose – just slower and more cumbersome.

Day to day odds and ends we would buy from the top shops in Poplar Road on the Batchley or from the Post Office. There was a whole range of small outlets at the top shops which still survive today although the occupants and types of shops have changed enormously. From memory there was a wool shop, butcher, sweet shop, chemist, furniture shop, cobblers, grocers, hardware/toy shop, newsagents (or paper shop as we called it), greengrocers and hairdressers. Apologies if I have missed any. If we needed anything then it would be me or Peter who were sent "down the shops." All shops closed for half a day on Wednesday afternoons and all day on Sundays. If we needed anything on those days we would be sent up to the post office, the grocery part of which was open every day.

Each Friday evening, on his way home from work, Dad would collect "the papers" from the newsagent. They would be rolled up and tied with raffia, and normally contained the local weekly *Redditch Indicator* for Dad, the *Beano, Dandy* or *Beezer* comics for us kids and a women's magazine, *Woman* or *Woman's Weekly,* for Mum plus a copy of the *Radio Times.* As the 60s rolled on, we would have the *Melody Maker* so we could keep up with the ever-changing music scene and the latest Top 20.

There was one occasion when I had been asked to go down the shops by Dad. He was doing some decorating in the house and had run out of undercoat. He knew that Whites, the hardware shop, sold what he wanted so he asked me if I would go and pick some up for him. Off I went, bought the paint and started back towards home, only about a 10 minute walk. What you must remember at this point is that all undercoat was oil-based, not water-based. So, small spillages and brushes had to be cleaned with turpentine or white spirit. Back to my journey home. I thought, in order to get the paint to Dad as quickly as possible, that I would run home – big mistake. I got to within sight of the house when I tripped and fell. The tin of undercoat paint, which incidentally was bright pink, flew through the air and landed on the pavement. Off popped the lid and there was nothing I could do to stop the paint from pouring out everywhere. In my panic I tried to scoop it back into the tin but only succeeded in getting as much on me as there was on the pavement. I arrived at the back door covered in paint and holding out the pot which, as Dad would say, "had less than a sore tooth full" left inside. There was nothing I could do or say to make the situation any better. Worse, the paint on the pavement could not be washed away with water so was simply left to dry. I can remember, years later, there still being flecks of pink paint there to remind me.

New potatoes were only available during spring when early potatoes were dug from the ground. It would have been unthinkable to eat them with the skins on. At the weekend, Dad would have the job of scraping the skins off. This was OK if they were "easy scrapers" but a real chore if they weren't. We would always have them boiled and they would be cooked with a sprig or two of mint in the saucepan.

One of my jobs would be to shell the peas from their pods when they were in season. I think I used to eat as many as I put in the pan. Another quirky story comes to mind – Mum used to boil the peas in water that had a little sugar added. Once tender, the water in which they had been cooked the "pea water" was drained into cups and we used to fight over who would have it to drink. It was absolutely delicious. I'm not sure if anyone else did this but it was something to really look forward to on a Sunday, almost the same pleasure as being able to scrape the cake bowl when Mum was baking.

I'm trying to think of some of the sweets and chocolates that were available at this time. Some of you will remember mint and fruit varieties of Spangles and Polos, chocolate Caramac, flying saucers, Spanish Gold which was a kind of sweet coconut wrapped up like tobacco, coloured kali (pronounced kay-lie) which was crystallised sherbet in layered colours, bought loose as one or two ounces in a paper bag and eaten by wetting your finger, dipping it in and licking the kali off. Fingers would remain coloured for days! Then there were sherbet fountains, iced gems, Fry's Five Boys chocolate which was filled with mint cream, and herbal tablets. Things such as Mars Bars, Milky Ways and Cadbury's Dairy Milk were also around but much more expensive. Biscuits were largely homemade, but we did have Lincoln biscuits which were pretty good for dunking in hot tea, providing that you didn't leave them in the tea for too long to the point where they fell in the drink and you were left with this "sludge" at the bottom! Most chocolate or special types of biscuits would only be available at Christmas in family boxes.

Darvill and Baker were a local company which produced lemonade, cherryade, orangeade and various other 'ades. They would come around the estate in their lorry and deliver pre-ordered bottles, known collectively as "pop," or you could just buy a bottle from the driver, the "pop-man." My favourite, though, was dandelion and burdock. I was never very clear about what it was really made from, but it was delicious, and very different to the same flavour sold today. Also, one paid a deposit on pop bottles which was refundable when you gave them back – not dissimilar to the "brand new policy" currently under discussion by Government in order to reduce plastic waste. We seem to be going full circle.

Talking of glass pop bottles, during the winter we had these filled with hot water to act as hot water bottles in our beds. Sometimes they were so hot that they would have to be wrapped in a pillowcase to stop us from burning our feet and legs. Can you imagine that these days!?

Another drinks delivery service at that time was Davenports. They were a Birmingham-based brewery who delivered various beers to order on a weekly basis. There was a TV advert with a little song that advertised the service and which I will never forget:

Beer at home means Davenports
That's the beer – lots of cheer.
The finest malt with hops and yeast
Turns your snack into a feast.
Straight from Brewery to your home,
Why collect, we'll deliver.
Soon you'll know why folks all say Beer at home means Davenports.
Cheers!

Chapter Nine

1965 to 1970

WHEN I was twelve years old it was back to hospital for me. I suffered each winter for years from tonsillitis, so the time came when the doctor decided that I should have my tonsils removed. This couldn't be carried out at Redditch hospital, so I had to go to the hospital at Bromsgrove. I think that I stayed in hospital for about a week, and everything went without a hitch. I mentioned earlier in the book about visiting Auntie Mabel and hating the caul or kell with which she wrapped faggots. I was to experience something far worse here in hospital. In those days, once one's tonsils were removed, you were only served

Bromsgrove Hospital, now demolished.

soft food. The good side of this was that I had ice cream every day for dessert. The horrible part was that, for my main evening meal, I was served with beef tripe. Now, for the uninitiated, beef tripe consists of the muscle wall of the first three chambers of a cow's stomach. It had the consistency of raw jelly and tasted awful. I was only allowed my ice cream if I ate the tripe, so I used to put small amounts in my mouth, let it slither around for a while and then swallow it quickly. I could never bring myself to chew it. Each swallowing was immediately followed by copious amounts of water!

September 1965 heralded the start of my "big school" days. I must say, right from the beginning, that I loved going to the County High School.

The school itself was split into three parts. The newer buildings housed the first and second years. The old part of the building, which was quite magnificent and dated from the 1930s, housed children in the third, fourth and fifth years. There was additionally a very modern block for the lower and upper sixth forms which was constructed when I was in the first year. The fact that the original school building was constructed in 1932 is quite scary in that it had only been opened for 33 years when I started there whereas it is over 50 years since I left!

The school has experienced several identity changes even in the relatively short period of time since I started there. The school began as the Redditch Secondary School when it first opened in 1932 before later becoming Redditch County High School – RCHS for short – a selection-driven grammar school with around 1,000 boys and girls, with 200 in the sixth form. The school operated a house system with three houses initially, Angles, Jutes and Saxons. A fourth house, Celts, was later added. Under a government reform of education, the grammar school became a comprehensive school in 1974 and was renamed the Abbey High School after the nearby ruins of Bordesley Abbey, continuing to operate the original house system. In 2001 the Abbey High School was closed and reopened as Trinity High School and Sixth Form Centre. In 2004, Trinity became a Business and Enterprise specialist school, and on 1 August 2011 Trinity became the first Independent State Funded Academy in Redditch.

I was lucky in that I already knew quite a few new starters who were transferring with me from Holyoakes Field. Nonetheless, this was a huge school which, in itself, made things quite daunting. It was not uncommon to lose one's way changing classrooms between lessons. In my previous schools we generally stayed in the same classroom regardless of the lesson and the same teacher mostly taught every subject. How dissimilar my new school was. Different classrooms and teachers for each subject, big science laboratories, art rooms, woodwork and metalwork shops, two gymnasiums, a huge hall that even had a balcony. No wonder it took some time to get familiar with everything.

The headmaster was Mr. Frank Chettle, a giant of a man, and Mr. Speed was the Deputy-Head. I was lucky enough never to have run-ins with either of them.

Then there were the school rules – some of which I recall breaking. These are the official copies:

REDDITCH COUNTY HIGH SCHOOL

RULES

1. Courteous behaviour is expected in and out of school. Pupils must be punctual. Movement about the school must at all times be in accordance with the rule: Keep to the left, walk in single file, do not run.
School property and premises must be respected. Children are responsible for their personal property, which must be clearly marked. Money and valuables must not be left in desks or cloakrooms. The Governors cannot accept responsibility for any loss or damage to personal belongings. Members of staff will undertake to look after personal property during practical lessons if requested.

2. Pupils are expected to keep the "Out-of-Bounds" rules which are issued from time to time. Those who remain for dinners must not leave the school grounds unless a written request from parent or guardian has been signed by the Headmaster or a member of staff. During the morning break and the dinner interval, pupils may use the Main Hall and the Dining Hall. The libraries are open to pupils in the dinner interval. In fine weather pupils should go out of doors.

3. No pupil should be absent, without permission from the Headmaster, for any reason other than illness. In the event of illness, a note should be sent within THREE DAYS; if the illness is infectious or contagious, notification should be sent at once. Permission for absence cannot be granted for merely social occasions.

4. Homework will be excused only if permission is obtained beforehand. If for some reason a pupil is unable to complete the homework set, a note of explanation must be sent.

5. Pupils must consume food only within the Dining Hall.

6. Prefects must be obeyed at all times, but pupils have a right to bring to the Headmaster an objection against what is felt to be unfair treatment.

7. If a detention is given, a pupil will not be expected to serve it until the following day at the earliest. If a pupil who is to serve a detention on a particular day finds it impossible to do so, he must obtain permission to postpone the detention either from the Headmaster or from the member of staff on duty.

8. Regulations with regard to clothing must be observed on all school occasions. If for some reason a pupil is unable to comply, a note of explanation must be sent. Girls are not allowed to use cosmetics, including nail varnish, or to wear jewellery.

9. Cycling in the school grounds is not allowed. Pupils are not permitted to park cars on the school grounds; permits for bringing motor bicycles, motor scooters or motorised cycles to school must be obtained from the Headmaster. Crash helmets must be worn by motor cyclists and pillion riders.

10. While smoking is the ultimate responsibility of the parents, it will not be allowed under any circumstances either on the school premises or on school outings or in school uniform.

N.B. The Headmaster reserves the right to amend the rules at any time, but in the case of a major alteration, it would first to considered by the Board of Governors.

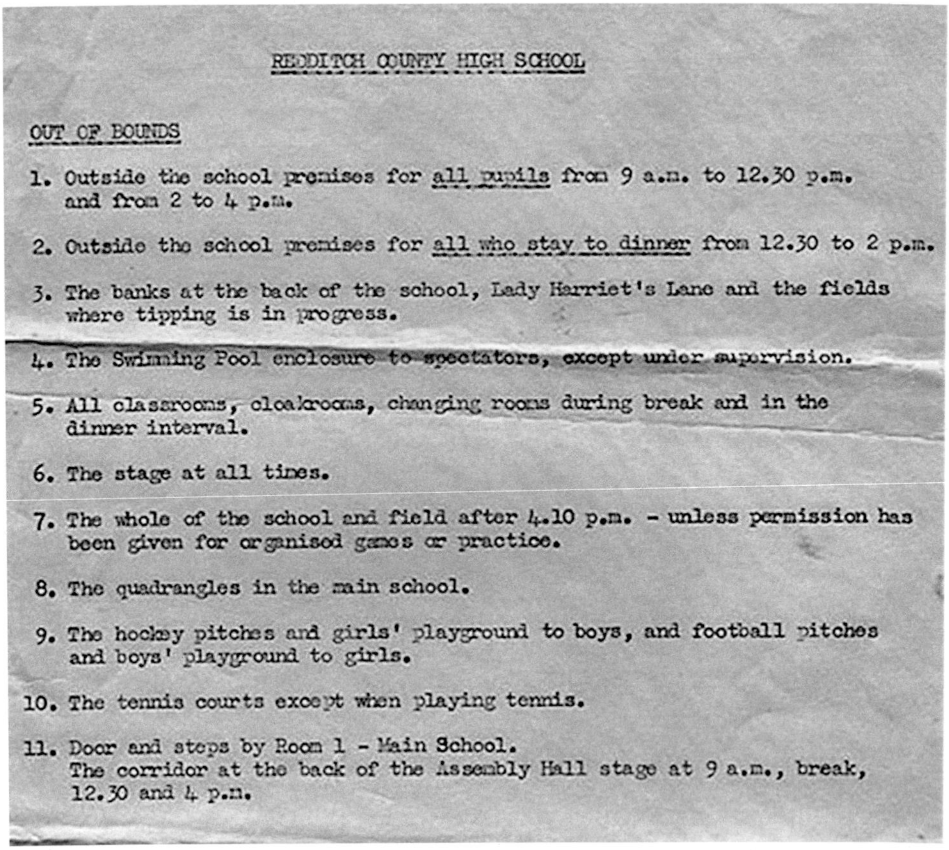

REDDITCH COUNTY HIGH SCHOOL

OUT OF BOUNDS

1. Outside the school premises for all pupils from 9 a.m. to 12.30 p.m. and from 2 to 4 p.m.

2. Outside the school premises for all who stay to dinner from 12.30 to 2 p.m.

3. The banks at the back of the school, Lady Harriet's Lane and the fields where tipping is in progress.

4. The Swimming Pool enclosure to spectators, except under supervision.

5. All classrooms, cloakrooms, changing rooms during break and in the dinner interval.

6. The stage at all times.

7. The whole of the school and field after 4.10 p.m. - unless permission has been given for organised games or practice.

8. The quadrangles in the main school.

9. The hockey pitches and girls' playground to boys, and football pitches and boys' playground to girls.

10. The tennis courts except when playing tennis.

11. Door and steps by Room 1 - Main School.
The corridor at the back of the Assembly Hall stage at 9 a.m., break, 12.30 and 4 p.m.

RCHS School Rules.

There was a system of detention for those who decided to transgress the rules which meant that on a given evening during the week, after school finished, one would have to go to an allocated classroom and carry out extra work for an hour.

I pride myself in a small way for never receiving a detention but in a much bigger way for never getting caught!

Day one was taken up with classroom, teacher and house allocation. Being sorted into the four houses bore more than a little resemblance to that we see in today's Harry Potter movies with the sorting hat. We were all put into the new gym and our names and houses were called out. All four houses existed by the time I started:

Angles – named after one of the main Germanic peoples who settled in Great Britain in the post-Roman period.

Saxons – named after a group of Germanic tribes first mentioned as living near the North Sea coast of what is now Germany (Old Saxony), in the late Roman Empire and which later invaded and populated part of Britain.

Jutes – another race which invade our islands and named after one of the three most powerful Germanic peoples of their time in the Nordic Iron Age.

Celts – were the Celtic-speaking peoples of the British and Irish islands and their descendants.

I fully expected to be put into the Angles house. This was the house that Peter was in, and it more often than not followed that siblings would be placed in the same house. However, because the Celts house was quite new this could not happen in such a well-oiled fashion. When my name was called it was for the Celts. Given that World War II had only ended a little over 20 years before I felt somewhat pleased that I ended up in a house that had no direct Germanic connections!

Each house had a colour:

Angles – Blue.

Saxons – Red.

Jutes – Yellow.

Celts – Green.

I think I was in the third year when the school tie was adapted into four versions, each version depicting an additional coloured stripe appropriate for the wearer's house.

As a first former there was always the danger that one would experience a degree of bullying from those in higher years. Although I encountered a little of this, I think that the fact of my older brother being in the fourth year offered me a little protection. Bless you, Peter!

I remember several teachers from the first two years. Mr. Agate used to teach Latin. In my view, he was a true bully although I expect that he thought he was just doing his job of teaching. Each week we would have a test. If someone got an answer wrong, they would have to stand up. Another incorrect answer meant they had to stand on their chair. More mistakes meant having to stand on the desk. Mr. Agate used to laugh about this but not in a nice way. Even when one of the girls slipped and fell from the desk one day, he just told her to get up and stop blubbering, despite the fact that she had hurt her leg quite badly.

Miss Best taught History, which I quite liked, although I must say I rather liked Miss Best as well. She was far more humane and compassionate with us pupils and she was very pretty.

Miss Jackson, my math's teacher, on the other hand was what I would call "old school." Short and rather stubby with dishevelled grey hair and very thin-framed glasses.

Eric Jones, "Jonah", was the head of sports. He could be very gruff, extremely firm, and brutally honest. Good or bad, you knew exactly where you stood with him. Like many newcomers to the school, he used to terrify me but, as I grew older, I came to respect him hugely.

During the winter months, probably a couple of times a month, we were sent for a cross-country run. This could be in any weather. Out of the school we would trot, and down Easemore Road before turning right into Lady Harriet's Lane. This took us through some quite boggy ground until we came to the River Arrow which we followed towards Abbeydale before turning back towards the school. I suppose it took about an hour to complete, although for those who, unlike me, didn't pause en route it would be more like forty minutes! We would invariably be covered in mud from head to foot by the time we got back. The changing room shower was always welcomed afterwards.

Being the mid-1960s, us boys were far more fashion-conscious than boys before us had ever been. I had begun to wear my hair much longer and used (I am almost ashamed to say) a male hair spray called Cossack to hold my hair in place.

Some years later – it was actually the year after I had left school – I went on a school ski-ing trip to the Tyrol region of Austria. Mr. Jones led the trip together with another teacher, Mrs Venables. Thinking about it, he and Mrs Venables always seemed to lead the school trips together! They took us camping in Snowdonia and canoeing to Hay-on-Wye in other years. Anyway, because I was no longer a pupil (I had joined West Mercia Constabulary as a Cadet), he treated me much more like an adult and we had some quite meaningful discussions about all sorts of things. I could never bring myself to call him Eric though. He was always either Mr. Jones or "sir"!

Miss Price was the General Science teacher, and I was convinced she disliked children so much that we would end up as part of one of her experiments! The science laboratory was on the top floor of one of the newer blocks. I remember that one of our class had a tiny radio that we would listen to on our way between classes. It would have been 1967 so I would have been approaching the end of the second year. As we were climbing the stairs to the lab there was a news bulletin about Israel having won the 6 days war against neighbouring Arab countries. It was very easy to wish oneself in the Middle East at that particular moment rather than having to encounter Miss Price!

Mr. Knowles was another PE teacher who also taught Geography. He was something of a hero-figure because he played football at the weekend for Alvechurch FC. Alvechurch was a very respectable amateur team who had several good runs in the FA Amateur Cup. I would often read about Mr. Knowles' performance from the match report in the *Sports Argus*. He was a good player but one Saturday he got sent off. Of course, we had Geography with him the following Monday morning but, somehow, he wasn't very keen on talking about the game that day!

Mr. Plimm, Danny Plimm, was an English teacher extraordinaire! He must have been in his late fifties but what a wonderful teacher of English, especially poetry. One of my favourite poems that he used to recite periodically was *Gungha Din* by Rudyard Kipling, but he used to read it in the voice and character of an East london-born working-class soldier. I loved it to the point whereby, some 50 years later, I recited the same poem in the very same fashion at a poetry evening at my local Parish Church.

The first two years at the High School passed by fairly quickly and without incident. It was in the third year that I started to develop an interest in something I would never have thought I would ever have done. I had never displayed much of an interest in thespian activities other than enjoying various programmes on the TV or in the cinema. I developed close friendships with several boys who were a couple of years older than me and who were involved in producing stage sets and lighting for school plays and operas. These were Alistair Law who lived in Birchfield Road opposite the junction with Feckenham Road, Geoff Osborne who lived further down Foxlydiate Crescent and Dave Jervis who was from the Webheath area. Before long they started involving me in the technicalities of stage lighting which I took to like a duck to water. Suddenly, I was involved in a world that included George Bernard Shaw, Gilbert & Sullivan and Benjamin Britten.... and I loved it. With operettas such as *The Mikado, The Pirates of Penzance* and *Cox & Box*, and plays like

Major Barbara, I found myself attending all the rehearsals and learning all the words. I never had any inclination to perform on the stage but it gave me, as one of the lighting and stage technicians, a real sense of belonging.

Most of the school performers and support workers were in the fifth or sixth form but I became almost a guest member of their group.

Alistair was a bit of a motorcycle buff but the modern Japanese makes were not for him. He had an old British Matchless machine. Matchless produced motorcycles in London but went out of business in 1967. Alistair's machine would only go about 50 miles an hour – but it would drive up the side of a house at 50 miles an hour! There were many occasions when I rode pillion on this – no helmet of course – and he would come to our house to pick me up although I am not sure that Mum and Dad entirely approved. Dave Jervis had a machine at the other end of the scale. He was the proud owner of a Honda 50 which, although called a motorcycle was little more than a glorified moped. Geoff obviously had a little more money because he owned a Mini car which, I seem to recall, spent more time off the road than on!

Many extra-curricular hours were spent at school during evening times designing lighting systems and trying different sets. In charge of all of this was Dave Griffin, one of the physics teachers. He was one of those teachers who always wanted to be "one of the boys" but couldn't be because of his position. He was, however, very different out of school hours, a really interesting and rather comical character who was much more part of the team rather than the lead. Most of the school productions would run for three nights – Thursday, Friday and Saturday – and always to a full house. The hall held around 1000 people, so it made for a very warm atmosphere.

Each Friday night of a show the local *Redditch Indicator* arts reporter, Mr. H K Kettle, would come along and we would wait with bated breath to read his review in the newspaper the following week. It was mainly very good and positive, but he never shied away from adding some constructive criticism if it was warranted.

Most of the productions, certainly each of the Gilbert and Sullivan operettas, were directed by the music teacher, Fred Morris – or Frederick Harvey Morris to give him his full name. Again, he was a teacher of his time – knew exactly what he wanted from the lead singers and chorus and would be very assertive in getting people to deliver. His favourite pupil, however, was

Cast of The Mikado *1968 – Felicity Barlow as Yum Yum in the front centre of the "Three Little Maids".*

Dress rehearsal for The Mikado *1968 – Yum Yum and Nanki-Poo showing their "affection" for one another! Rear view of director, Fred Morris, conducting the school orchestra.*

Felicity Barlow. She also lived in Foxlydiate Crescent and, as well as being very attractive, was an excellent singer. She would always be chosen to play the leading girl. For instance, in *The Mikado* she played the role of Yum Yum (one of the "three little maids from school"). It was quite amusing that her "love interest" on stage was the King's son, Nanki-Poo, who, disguised as the "Wandering Minstrel," pledged his love for Yum Yum. To cut another long story short, one scene involved them embracing and passionately kissing. This would have been fine but for the fact that Felicity really couldn't stand the actor playing opposite her and for all the flirting and smiling and kissing on stage, they struggled to speak with one another off stage!

Party after the last performance of Major Barbara in 1967. Held in the main gym. L to R Unknown, Mr. Murray the woodwork teacher, Dave Griffin, Geoff Osborne, Me, Gareth Jones. On floor, Keith Williams.

After the final performance of every production, which would always fall on a Saturday night, there was always a big party for the performers, orchestra, technicians and staff. This tended to start off with sandwiches, crisps and soft drinks but very quickly advanced into what could best be termed an "alcoholic evening." No-one ever got blindingly drunk but several gallon containers of scrumpy cider from the Waggon and Horses pub up the road would appear and be imbibed.

It is something of a coincidence that Keith Williams, one of the backroom team for the production of *Major Barbara*, would, in years to come, become the brother-in-law of Jane Fowkes. Small world or what!

Earlier in 1967 I went on a school trip to West Malvern Field Centre. This lasted for a school week – 5 days – and was designed to increase knowledge, and practical experience through experiments, of fieldwork that was being

West Malvern Field Centre.

carried out with plants and trees. The place itself had used to be an open-air school where children who had respiratory health problems would be sent as full boarders for several months in order that fresh air could assist in helping them recover. When I was five or six years old, I remember Martin, who suffered badly from asthma, being sent there for three or four months to help him overcome this problem. Mum and Dad were not allowed to visit him for several weeks although they, and Martin, were encouraged to write letters. This school trip therefore had a greater significance for me than for all the other pupils. The main difference between when Martin was there and my trip was that, in Martin's day, the windows had no glass in them, only wooden slats. This helped in ensuring that he breathed in plenty of clean, fresh air. Suffice to say that when I stayed there, glass windowpanes were definitely in place!

My love of photography began at the Grammar School. When I was in the 5th Year, I discovered that the school had its own darkroom for developing films and printing photographs. One had to get permission to use it and obtain the key from the school secretary's office. This was just a standard Yale-type key, so I very quickly got myself a copy cut!

I spent many lunch breaks in the darkroom working on different aspects of "real" photography. Unlike the digital images of today, photographs were taken on a roll of light-sensitive film that one inserted into the back of the camera. That was the easy bit. Once the film had been used, I had to remove it in the darkroom, either in total darkness or with the help of a special red light which did not damage the exposed film. The film was removed from its canister and placed into a chemical solution called "developer." After a given amount of time the film would have been "developed" into negatives then hung up to dry. When completely dry you could load the negative into an enlarger which shone an image of the negative downwards onto a piece of light-sensitive photographic paper. The paper would be exposed to the image for a few seconds then it was placed into the developer. Under the red light you could then see the image appear. Once complete, the paper would be put into another chemical solution called "fixer" which would make the image permanent. Once done and the paper was dried, you had your photograph!

I also quickly learned that the darkroom was a great place in which to hide especially for those boys who might be inclined to disappear in there for half an hour or so with one of the girls. Because I had a key, this became something of a money-making scheme for me. It's surprising how much people will pay for half an hour of privacy!

The school also had its own outdoor swimming pool in which lessons were taught and a gala held each year. This was built as a water tank for the school in the late 1930s and not converted into a pool until the mid-1950s. Well, the thought of a nice enjoyable outdoor swim in the spring and summer sunshine could not be further from the truth. The water was cold, incredibly cold, all year round and students would try anything to avoid swimming lessons (I think about the darkroom again here – ker-ching!). Normally when you get into a cold pool, such as Redditch Swimming baths that used to be in Hewell Road, the body gets used to it quite quickly and you can comfortably swim around. Not in this pool. Firstly, it was big – about two thirds the size of an Olympic pool with a depth that ranged from 3 feet to 12 feet. That is a huge amount of water for limited sun exposure to heat up and, of course, and there being no other means of heating, it never happened. It was quite common for people to get cramp whilst in the water. Although I enjoy swimming, like many of the others, if I could avoid the pool then I would.

Playing football and cricket were other loves of mine at the school. I represented the school at both in all years including the First XI. I was also awarded my colours for representing for Redditch District and Worcestershire County at football.

We used to have an all-weather clay pitch which we called the "red-grahh." I suppose that this name started life as "red-grass." It was a great surface on which to play but evil for slide-tackling or falling over. We tended to play in tracksuit bottoms, which reminds me of Tom Graveney's sports shop in Alcester Street. Tom was a first-class Test cricketer who played for Worcestershire and England for many years during the 50s and 60s. He took on the shop which was where I would buy all my football boots. My favourite boots of the day were Adidas Santiago which had screw-in studs, something very new, and were really comfortable to wear. To coin a phrase from Henry Ford in 1903 about his Ford Model T motor car, you could have the boots in any colour you like as long as they were black! (Unlike the rainbow array of coloured boots or "football slippers" that modern footballers use). One Christmas I remember Mum and Dad buying me a tracksuit from the shop. Tom would often be serving and would be more than happy to sign autographs, which he did on the box.

On May 6th 1967, Peter and I went to the Odeon Theatre in Birmingham to watch the Beach Boys. Peter tells a story here. He had told his girlfriend of the time that he had two tickets to go and watch the group. She, by now quite excited, expected him to say that they were for him and her. She must have been quite crestfallen when he said "No, me and our kid are going!"

This was a fabulous once-in-a-lifetime concert for me although the band performed without the legendary Brian Wilson. Wilson was going through a bad period in his life and had decided he was no longer going to tour with the band, so they brought in another legend, Glen Campbell, as a temporary replacement for the UK tour. Value for money or what! The band wore their instantly recognisable blue and white wide stripe, short-sleeved shirts and white trousers. *Good Vibrations* had not long been released and they played it live. It was pretty amazing to be able to recreate the electronic sounds of the record live on stage. I also remember that the supporting acts included Helen Shapiro (*Walkin' Back to Happiness*) and Simon Dupree and the Big Sound (*Kites*).

Beach Boys Tour of the UK 1967.

I used to belong to an organisation called the Redditch Society in my mid-teens. There was a group of us from the school that joined up. The Society met every month on a Friday evening at Redditch College of Further

Education. I am not altogether sure whether or not the organisation still exists, although it might now be the Redditch History Society, but its aim when I was a member was to present talks and lectures on a variety of topics from the fields of science, literature and the arts. These would be delivered by well-known figures from the town and outside. Each event, some of which would be illustrated by a slideshow, would be attended by fifty or so people and was a real social evening.

As I neared the end of my school days, I really didn't have any idea as to what direction my life would take by way of a career. I had been to several school career interviews, and I was told about working in a bank and other things which really didn't fill me with a great deal of enthusiasm. One evening there was a career convention at the school but for one reason or another I couldn't go. One of my friends did though, and he brought back some leaflets, one of which was all about joining the Police Force as a Cadet. This would be a full-time paid job for 2 years until I was old enough to join as a Constable. I liked the look of this, and, after a number of examinations and interviews, I was selected to join West Mercia Constabulary Cadets in 1970. Although I was fully supported by both Mum and Dad, I think they were both a little disappointed that I didn't go into the family business, ASGO Sheet Metal Ltd. This meant that none of us three boys went into the business. Do I regret not doing so? I am certainly sorry for causing Mum and Dad disappointment but once I was in The Job (as the Police Force was, and still is, referred to by serving officers in the UK), I never looked back.

My last week at school I found quite upsetting and almost traumatic. It suddenly occurred to me that I was about to leave all of my friends behind, that I would never again feel that pleasure of being at school and that I was about to be thrown into a new world that I knew nothing about. This was all very scary.

A couple of days before the school broke off, all students went to St Stephen's Church in the town centre for the Leavers Service. I remember singing the school hymn *Nil Nisi Optime* – Latin: Nothing but the best – with tears rolling down my cheek. It sounds crazy now but that is how I felt about leaving. On the day of leaving, it was even worse. Lots of people crying, saying their good-byes to colleagues and teachers. It is often said that school days are the best days of your life. It was only after I had left that I realised just how true this is. How wonderful it would be to have an old head on young shoulders!

So, off I went never to return, with the summer holiday ahead of me and the Police Force beckoning. From school uniform to that of West Mercia Constabulary. But that is another story for another day.

Police Cadet Aston at West Mercia Police College, Droitwich – 1970.

Chapter Ten

The Fowkes Family

THE FOWKESES were our next-door neighbours, at 117 Foxlydiate Crescent. Although before I was born, I am guessing that they moved in more or less at the same time that Mum, Dad, Martin and Peter did, when the houses had not long been built. Mr. and Mrs. Fowkes were only, and always, what I was allowed to call them. Even Mum used to call them Mr. and Mrs. rather than their first names which were Reginald (Reg) and Dorothy. Dad knew Mr. Fowkes (even now, I can't bring myself to call him Reg) from many years earlier. In the 1930s they and their friends would drink together at the Plumbers Arms in Walford Street where Mr. Fowkes would play the piano. I remember him having a moped, a Raleigh I think, on which he travelled to work every day. I would often watch him ride off down the Crescent. I never knew why but every single morning he would stop a couple of hundred yards down the yard, only for a few seconds, and then move off again. This was, and still is, a complete mystery to me as to why this might have been!

They had two daughters, Margaret and Jane. Jane was a year older than me, being born in September 1952. Margaret was four years older.

From the outset, Margaret, Jane and I became firm friends, and remained very close until they moved from the Batchley to Cedar Road in the early 1960s. When I was 3 and Jane was 4, we were almost inseparable, particularly because Margaret had already started school and so, as playmates, we had only each other.

One's memory can sometimes distort reality and, when I look back, every day seemed to be sunny and dry. Of course, that couldn't have been the case but nonetheless, we had wonderful but simple and innocent times together. We would play in each other's gardens, wander through the field at the back of our houses (where Monks Path was later built) and play in the woods. Quite simply, Jane was the first best friend I ever had. I can recall being totally devastated when she became 5 years old and started school. I could not believe, even at that age, that I would no longer be able to play with her during the day in the week. I remember continually asking Mum what the time was and when Jane would be home after school.

Holiday times and weekends were very special because we would all get together. "All" included several other children from the Crescent. We had a small gang including me, Margaret, Jane, Corinne Green from No 125 and sometimes Bernie McDermott from over the road at 148, Diane and Teresa Hughes from 127, an English/Polish boy, Jurek Wydrynski, who lived with his family at 119 and Susan Morgan from Pine Tree Close.

Picnic in the back garden of the Fowkeses garden, 117, circa 1960. L-R Susan Morgan, Jane Fowkes, Corinne Green, Margaret Fowkes, Bernie McDermott and Me.

Margaret and Jane's back garden seemed to be the favoured venue in which to play. On hot summers days we would enjoy making a tent which basically consisted of an upturned wooden clothes horse with a blanket thrown over the top, but this would be our den.

When it was really hot we used to borrow a galvanised metal washing tub from Mrs Fowkes, fill it with water, then get a dining room chair which we put next to the tub and then take turns to jump from the chair into the tub. We would have picnics on the lawn. Our respective Mums would make us some sandwiches and drinks and we would have a wonderful time.

We would also play "Mums and Dads." The tent would be the main room and then we would build imaginary walls and door using line-props and the like to mark out the boundaries. All these games must sound very modest and humble compared to the vast array of electronic games and gadgetry available today, but we used our imaginations, made up games and created memories that, for me, have lasted a lifetime.

I think it was Margaret who, one year, became the proud owner of a small green bicycle. This could have been a hand-me-down from one of her cousins. Albeit small, this was a proper bike with no stabilisers and a single brake. I remember that the gang used to take turns riding, or learning to ride, the bike. We used to ride from the Fowkeses' garden gate, down the footpath, past Corinne's house, for about 100 yards to a small patch of grass, then ride back again. It took me ages to conquer the art of cycling. More often than not, I would end up having a helpful push at the start, wobbling all the way down the path, and being grateful for the grass patch that I could fall on when I reached it without too much risk of injury!

If the weather was bad, we would sometimes congregate in Margaret and Jane's garden shed. The sheds that belonged to the houses were quite large, probably 20 feet long and 8 feet wide, built with pre-formed concrete slats and an asbestos corrugated roof. There was an area set aside for coal at one end and the rest was available for storage. Storage normally consisted of bikes, tools, benches and anything else for which there was no place in the house. We formed a club at one point which I'm sure would have been influenced by Enid Blyton's *Secret Seven* novels and we used to meet in the shed. I seem to remember that, at one point, we even had badges which, if my memory serves me correctly, were made by Mrs Fowkes and which consisted of a small round piece of leather material affixed to our clothing with a hairgrip. I don't think that the club ever had a name, nor do I recall that it lasted for a huge amount of time, probably only through one summer, but it was another example of how we created our own games and entertainment.

Some weekends we were allowed into Corinne Green's house. She had a whole collection of Cliff Richard records – *The Young Ones, Please Don't Tease, A Girl Like You* – and many more. We would sit and play them over and over. I remember that they were on the Columbia label which, during that period, was coloured green. The first Cliff hits, *Move it* and *Travelin' Light* were issued on the Columbia brown label, and, in later years, the label became green, then black. Just one of those geeky bits of trivia!

As with any close group of friends, we would sometimes and inevitably, have a falling out. Even this was ritualised. Members of the gang would make sure that whomever were those who had fallen out with each other, really wanted to "break up," following which the adversaries would shake hands and chant "Break friends, break friends, never, never make friends." They would then go their separate ways. As with most children, this never lasted very long. In a very short time, sometimes even the same day, the gang would reconvene, and a similar ritual would be carried out but this time the chant would be "Make friends, make friends, never, never break friends." All would be well again.

The times with Margaret and Jane were the best and it was a massive blow to learn that they were to move out of Foxlydiate Crescent into Cedar Road which was a bus journey away. I am guessing that this would have been around 1962/63 when I was 9 or 10 years old. This seemed like the end of the world for me and there were many tears shed leading up to the day they left.

I visited them a few times at their new home, a bungalow, and sometimes took our portable record player with me to play records. The Valley Stadium, home of Redditch Football Club, was at the bottom of their garden and sometimes, on a Saturday afternoon, we would climb out of the back of the garden at the rear of the old, covered terrace to watch the Reds play for free. Margaret and Jane, at other times, would watch the football from high up in a tree in their garden. Mr. Fowkes, on the other hand, would always walk round to the turnstiles and pay to get in. Sadly though, that era of close daily friendship had drawn to a close and we all went our separate ways.

Without either me or they knowing it, Margaret and Jane – Jane especially because she was nearer my age – taught me huge amounts about friendships, loyalty, honesty, fairness and trusting. Looking back, I have huge admiration for both of them and value their friendships enormously. They helped to shape my childhood into the happiest of times. I will never forget that.

Chapter Eleven

My Redditch

THE TOWN centre of Redditch I remember as a child was nothing whatsoever like the centre of today. The town had a population of some 25,000 and its main industries were still fishing tackle, needles and springs.

Today, over 50 years after the commencement of the New Town construction and approaching 60 years after the New Town plan was first published, the town has grown to a population a little short of 90,000 with a central area that bears little resemblance to the town I knew and loved.

For me, the main part of the old town was The Cross which was the crossroads that joined Evesham Street, Marketplace, Church Green West and Unicorn Hill together. Evesham Street and Marketplace were the main shopping areas with Alcester Street not far behind.

Evesham Street stretched from The Cross all the way to Mount Pleasant and Evesham Road. It was full of shops of all sorts on both sides of the road. Many of these were one-off independently owned shops rather than the conglomerates of today. There was no one-way system in the town until the late 1960s and the building of the New Town a little later.

Although I am jumping forwards a tad to 1971 (which I know is marginly outside the parameters of this book), I can't resist telling you about a competition in which I became involved that only a very few, and select, people even knew existed. I was a police cadet stationed at Redditch Police Station in Church Road. Firstly, you need to understand that there is nothing worse than a bored policeman on nights. Redditch was not exactly sin city and, after midnight, it would be most unusual for anything at all to warrant the attendance of the police. In those days, as part of the newly introduced Unit Beat Policing, mobile "Panda" patrols were used in order to make police responses and patrols more effective. West Mercia Constabulary used fleets of British Leyland Mini Countryman and Clubman estates as its "Panda" cars. The night shift would often put out three or four of these in the town plus the town centre foot patrols. This was right at the beginning of the building of the New Town and one of the first constructions was a multi-storey car park which led out, before other buildings had been started, into Evesham Street. The car park itself was, more or less, complete but there were no barriers or controls in place, so it was decided that it would be a good idea to inject a little excitement into the night. All the Pandas would assemble on the top floor then, in neutral gear, each one would start rolling down the ramps. Any braking was met with instant disqualification. The cars moved quite slowly at first but by the time they reached the exit, five floors down, they were going at some lick! Straight out onto the road at the exit, the object, still in neutral with no braking, being to get as far as possible before the vehicle eventually, and naturally came to a halt. On a good run it was possible to come whizzing down the ramps, turn left into Evesham Street, left again at The Cross (regardless of the colour of the traffic lights, but with the blue light flashing if they were on red!), and, if you were *really* lucky, all the way down Unicorn Hill to the railway station and beyond. We had hours of fun, even me with only a provisional driving licence and unaccompanied! Did I say that out loud?! Nights suddenly became the most attractive of shifts!

Back to pre-New Town days. Evesham Street held the greatest number and the most variety of shops. On Saturdays, there were also two open-air markets – one at the back of the Royal Hotel (where one of the fun fairs used to be during the carnival) and the other in a big car park opposite the fire station in Red Lion Street. Both were traditional markets with all sorts of stalls and that special atmosphere and smell that one always experiences with fresh vegetable stalls and the stallholders calling out to shoppers and to each other with their unique banter. My cousin Warwick Humphries, Auntie Mabel's son, worked on Redditch market for many years.

I will talk about the shops that meant something to me at the time. I mentioned earlier about Hollingtons and its Christmas toy shop but that was the only time of year that I would go there. Huins was a shoe shop at The Cross on the corner of Evesham Street and Market Place. As you walked in the door there was a machine with which you could see an x-ray image of your feet. You poked your feet into the gap at the bottom, pressed a button and, hey presto, an x-ray of your feet showing all the bones would appear. It was designed to get the best possible fit of shoe but the radiation risk of taking an infinite number of x-rays like this was simply not recognised. Great fun though!

There were two chemist shops in Evesham Street, Boots and a little further down, Timothy Whites & Taylors (which was later bought out by Boots). Mum worked for some years in Timothy Whites and then Boots. This reminds me of a story she told me. She was serving one day when a middle-aged man with a broad Welsh accent came in and asked for some "Urex." Mum, not being used in those days to openly selling anything to do with birth control, asked him to repeat what he wanted which he did – "Urex." Trying to remain professional she asked him what sort he would like. "What have

Mum (bottom left) with staff members at Boots the Chemist (formerly Timothy Whites & Taylors Chemist) circa 1966.

you got?" he replied. She reached underneath the counter (because this was where condoms lived in those days) and produced a variety of Durex packs. She laid out different sorts on the counter and asked which one he would like. At this the man became somewhat animated, pointed to his ears and, in his heavy Welsh brogue, said "No, Urex, Urex, to unblock my urs!!" It was only then Mum realised that the required merchandise was actually Earex! She was so embarrassed and, of course, many of her particularly younger female colleagues had witnessed this and were roaring with laughter. It was many weeks before Mum lived that one down.

In between the two chemist shops was W&R Fletcher, the butcher. Both Peter and I had part-time jobs there at different times, normally on a Saturday but sometimes after school as well. The shop was managed by a rather portly, and normally jovial, man called Sam. He had bright ginger hair and a short temper to match. There were two other men working there called Chris and Lee together with a lady whose name I forget.

My first job on Saturday morning was to make the beefburgers. This was done inside an annex room that was in the back yard. I would be given all the ingredients which I would have to put through an industrial mincer. I could not believe the sort of things that went into the burgers; scraps of beef that had been cut from joints, lumps of fat, bacon, bits of chicken – anything at all that could be minced down.

W&R Fletcher ("Sam's") where I used to work part-time.

To call them "beef" burgers was something of a misnomer and would definitely breach all manner of rules and regulations today but, I tell you what, people used to love them. We couldn't make enough. They were all gone by mid-morning and people would be putting orders in for the following Saturday. Once all the ingredients had been minced down, I would add the seasoning. This was a somewhat sinister-looking pinkish grey powder that I would add by the handful, and which lived inside a big cardboard box. Although I wore a white coat this was often covered in bits and blood from handling meat earlier and there were no such thing as protective gloves to wear. The huge bowl of now minced and seasoned material was ready to be converted into burgers. This was done manually using a press, so I could only make one at a time. A round piece of cellophane in the bottom, then some mixture, topped with another cellophane circle and pressed down. One made, something like another ninety-nine to go!

After the burgers it was time for me to go on the rounds and deliver meat to people's homes. I was given an old bicycle with a huge wicker basket on the front to accomplish this task. There were no gears, just the pedals and a single brake. Sam or one of the others would wrap up the deliveries and write on each one the address to which I had to take it. They would all be placed into

A typical butcher boy's bicycle from the 1950s and 1960s.

the basket which, to start the journey was very heavy, and off I would go. I used to deliver all over the place, Batchley, Abbeydale, Mayfields, Webheath and elsewhere. This would take the best part of three hours (except for one occasion in heavy snow when I did not arrive back at the shop until half past four!). In the main people were very cheerful and pleased to receive their order. There was one woman in Abbeydale, though, who would never believe that what she received was the weight that she had ordered. So, I would have to wait at her door whilst she weighed everything, even pre-packed chickens, on her scales. I used to dread going to her house.

She would often ring Sam while I was waiting and complain about either the quality or quantity then, of course, as the "messenger," she would verbally have a go at me. I couldn't get away fast enough!

Doing the rounds at Christmas was always good because I would make a hefty profit from the tips that customers gave to me. No surprise, I never got anything from the Abbeydale lady!

During busy periods I would serve on the counter. I was quite good at cutting, weighing and wrapping meat but the till always provided me with something of a challenge. It was an old manual till with large lever keys to press down and which raised a piece of plastic in the window on the top with the price on it. I could never get this right and often had to be rescued! There was a way that one could press the levers down halfway then, with the final press, all the "half – pressed" levers would go down together and the grand total would appear in the window. Again, not something that I readily grasped. Also, I used to get confused if the price came to, for instance, £2 1s 6d (just under £2 and 8p in today's money). A customer might say "would you like the odd 1/6d to save your change?", I would say no because I hadn't a clue as to how I would manage this on the till. Once more, Sam to the rescue!

The sort of cash register I used to use at the butcher.

The worst jobs of the day were cleaning which were my late afternoon tasks. I would be directed to the sink which was in a very tiny alcove, and which was used for everything from cleaning bloodied trays, to washing your hands to making tea and coffee. In the sink, an old crock and cracked butler type, I would be confronted by thirty or more trays that had previously held all sorts of meat and offal. They all needed to be cleaned ready for use on the following Monday. The only source of hot water was an ancient gas geyser that had clearly seen better days. There was never any sort of cleaning fluid so all the trays, one by one, were held beneath the running, fairly luke-warm, water and scrubbed clean with either an old dishcloth or with my fingers. They were then dried with a tea-towel that, before long, was itself soaking wet and filthy. At the end of the day all the trays looked clean and dry, but goodness knows what bacteria they still harboured. We never had any complaints from the customers about any illnesses though!

The other thing to be cleaned was the wooden butcher's block. This was where meat was cut and sliced and, through each day, became covered with soaked-in blood. The block must have been 10 – 12 inches in depth and simply trying to wipe it clean with cloths just did not work. It was necessary to get a brush that had very rigid steel teeth and, quite literally, scrub away the top layer of wood so that there was no blood left on the block. I knew when this job was coming up, so I used to try and hide. I was not sufficiently physically strong in those days to get enough "uumph" to remove any wood. It always ended up with one of the "grown-ups" finishing the block.

About once a month the large walk-in fridge had to be cleaned up and I would sometimes be given this job. It was freezing cold, and it didn't help when Lee, who was something of a joker, used to close the door on me! There was no handle on the inside so I would just have to wait it out until someone realised that I was still in there!

It was nothing unusual to be the subject of practical jokes. I can remember being dispatched into the town to buy a left-handed screwdriver (gullible or what!). Peter will talk of the time he was sent to buy something completely unaware that he had a pig's tail hanging from the bottom of his white coat!

The best part of the day was just before closing. This was when I got paid. For a full Saturday I used to be paid £1 10s 0d (£1 and 50 pence) which, to me, was a small fortune. In addition, Sam also would often give me a load of

Old Redditch public library on the corner of Church Green West and Church Road.

tins of fruit or soup that had become battered and could not be sold. If there were none in that state, he would drop a few on the floor! I was always a happy bunny going home, and so was Mum when I got there!

On the other side of The Cross was Church Green West which led down to the public library and Smallwood Hospital. There were underground ladies and gent's toilets along here, entry to which was via steep steps which became very slippery if it was raining. Daylight was provided downstairs through some very thick, opaque glass tiles upon which people walked above your head. The toilets were invariably very smelly. It was the case where, in order to get into a cubicle, you had to insert a penny into the door mechanism in order for it to open. This is where the expression "spending a penny" comes from many years before. Further along Church Green West was the Redditch Benefit Building Society and then, across the junction with Church Road, the library. I used to love visiting here. I have always been an avid reader, so this was a natural draw for me. The system of borrowing books was usual for the time but archaic by modern standards.

Every book contained a cardboard ticket which sat in a small envelope inside the front cover. One would select three or four books and take them to the counter. The tickets would be removed and placed against your name in a huge manual paper filing system. A slip of paper in each book would be stamped with the date by which it must be returned. Off you went with your books. If you returned a book later than the date stamp, then you would be fined something like a penny a day. This would have to be paid in cash with the coins being inserted through a slot into an old wooden box.

The Gaytime Cafe.

Just down the road at the junction of Evesham Street with Worcester Road was a café called the Gaytime. One must remember that the word "gay" in those days had no more meaning than being happy and enjoying life rather than the context in which it is used today. I would be sent to the café by Sam at the butcher's mid-morning on a Saturday to collect our orders of bacon and egg sandwiches. We would all have a double round, that is, four slices of bread with whatever we wanted inside. They were so delicious! The Gaytime was the sort of coffee bar that attracted young teenagers because it had a juke box inside with all of the latest hits. In the 1950s it would have been called a milk-bar because it did not sell alcohol. The youngsters that went in there would often either have "frothy" coffee or Coca-Cola.

Talking of music, one of the most popular shops in town was Spencer's. This was the only true record shop in the town where one could go and buy vinyl records of any genre, classic, pop, old-time, anything.

A TV western that was shown in the 50s and 60s was *Rawhide*. I loved the theme song to it, and it became the first record that I ever bought from Spencer's. It cost me 7s 6d (38p today) and was sung by Frankie Layne on the Phillips label. The first LP I bought was by the Bee Gees called *Bee Gees 1st* at a time when, in addition to the three Gibb brothers, the band also consisted of guitarist Vince Melouney and drummer Colin Peterson.

Spencer's Record Shop in Evesham Street.

Alcester Street had an eclectic array of shops but there were three that I remember well. The first one was Regents Coaches. Firstly with Peter and then more on my own, I would go to watch Aston Villa play at Villa Park (although I later became a firm bluenose Birmingham City fan!). I would go into Regents during the week to book my coach ticket. The coach would leave at Saturday lunchtime in time for the 3pm kick-off. When we arrived, the coach dropped us off near to the ground and then drive off to park in the coach park. We then queued up to pay through the turnstiles. Unless you wanted a seat in the stand there was none of this having to pre-buy a ticket. You just queued up and paid your 2s 6d (12 and a half pence) to get in. A programme cost 6d (2 and a half pence) and you could stand wherever you wanted to in the ground. It was not unusual for fans to congregate behind the goal into which their team was trying to score in the first half, then walk to be at the opposite end in the second half, After the final whistle at 4.40pm it was always a rush to get out of the ground and find the coach so that we would be able to listen to *Sports Report* at 5pm on the coach radio and hear all of the day's football results and reports. Believe it or not, *Sports Report* started its radio slot on 3rd January 1948 and, with the exception of a short and unwelcome break in the 1970s, has used the same theme music throughout. Those football fans reading this will now be hearing that tune in their heads!

When I was a little older, probably 14 or so, Jurek Wydrynski and I used to go to Old Trafford to watch Manchester United. He was a big United fan, but it was always a thrill for me to watch famous players such as Bobby Charlton, Denis Law and George Best in their prime. We would catch the train from Redditch to Birmingham then change onto the Manchester Piccadilly train from where it was a short walk to the ground. We wouldn't get back home until 10 or 11 o'clock that night.

We always took sandwiches and a flask of hot tea, which we would eat and drink on the train. I had another little moment one time when I was drinking a full cup of tea but decided I didn't want any more, so I opened the carriage window and threw the contents out. Of course, the train was travelling very quickly and the tea transported itself – at the same speed – along the side of the train and straight through the, also open, window in the next carriage compartment. I could hear the commotion next door and was so thankful that this was a no-corridor train, each compartment in the carriage was completely self-contained with doors either side to get on and off. When we got to Manchester, we got off the train so quickly and ran so as not to be accosted by our next-door occupants!

I digress once again! The next shop in Alcester Street was Fairest. This shop had a wonderful collection and display of toys. It specialised in train sets such as the Hornby 00 series, and in construction kits such as Airfix. I spent many a Saturday gazing through the window willing everything on the other side to magically become mine.

The third shop I remember was just past a Chapel further down from the junction with Grove Street. This was Roberts. It sold and hired televisions and radios. At various times we hired both from here and either with Mum, or

Mum sending me, I used to go there to pay the weekly rental to Mr. Roberts, a big jovial man.

I think that one of the big things I remember about old Redditch, which is very different today, is that you knew many of the people you passed in the town streets and they knew you. One could almost call Redditch intimate. Not so today.

The main shop in Market Place was, of course, Woolworths. This was the "shop of the people" and seemed to sell just about anything. It was a magical emporium, but what I loved best about it was what I called the broken biscuit counter. Biscuits were sold loose by weight and were displayed in large tins. It was inevitable that some would get broken and for about fourpence you could get a huge bag of broken biscuits, often with many that were unbroken. In those days Woolworths also sold single vinyl records, usually 45s, but only those on its own label – Embassy. The songs they sold were all modern but never by the original artists, always by people one had never heard of!

Whilst we are talking about money this is an opportune time to show you what coins and banknotes in the 1960s looked like:

British Coins of the 1950s and 1960s. Note that the shilling was minted in both English and Scottish versions. Crowns such as the one here commemorating Sir Winston Churchill were only issued on special occasions. All coins had the head of Queen Elizabeth II on the obverse.

Brown ten shillings note from the 1960s.

Green one pound note from the 1960s.

Blue five pounds notes from the 1960s.

Dark brown ten pounds notes from 1960s.

I don't recall ever seeing a £10 note as a child!

Saturdays at the Gaumont was great fun. Imagine a cinema ground floor filled to the brim with around 500 children aged between 5 and 12 – these were never going to be quiet occasions. The show followed a regular pattern – it started with a couple of cartoons (kids fairly quiet), then came a short film, often from the *Look at Life* documentary series which showed people at work both locally and nationally (boredom factor high so audience found alternative entertainment which often involved climbing over seats and fighting).

The weekly serial came next which would be something like *Batman and Robin, Captain Video* or the *Cisco Kid* (total silence – this was for *real*). The feature film would be on last and the behaviour in the auditorium would depend upon the film being shown.

Sometimes, before the films started there would be some sort of live entertainment. It must have been around 1965 when a local beat group called The Spartans would come and play the hits of the day. They were the "new style" of group, lead guitar, rhythm guitar, bass guitar and drums. They wore their hair long and had collarless jackets on. At least two of the band – the Bott brothers, or they could have been cousins, were from the town. The club cost, I think, sixpence to get in and I would have another sixpence to spend on sweets.

The Gaumont Cinema, Church Street.

A couple of times a year, when the weather was good, Mum and Dad would take us to the playing fields at Astwood Bank. These days, in a car, the journey from Foxlydiate to Astwood Bank takes less than 10 minutes. With

The family with Auntie Pam at Astwood Bank playing fields.

no car and having to take two buses to get there, it took us the best part of an hour and a half. This was a real treat for us, especially as we would take a picnic with us. There was nothing special about the park itself, but it did have a good slide, a roundabout and a witch's hat. We sometimes took a plastic football so that we could have a kickabout with Dad. Sometimes Auntie Pam and Uncle Eric would come with us and other times Granny and Grandad. It would be a proper day out.

It is interesting, almost ironic, that as I write parts of Redditch New Town built only in the 1970s and 80s are already in the planning stage of demolition. Indeed, some buildings have even now disappeared. Not, I believe, a great legacy from the vision of 1950s and 60s planners and architects.

Chapter Twelve

ASGO Sheet Metal Co Ltd

THIS STORY starts in 1968 and spills over into the 1980s.

ASGO was the brainchild of Dad and a workmate, Trevor Goode, who decided during the Spring of 1968 that they would form their own sheet metal fabrication and welding company. They had both worked for other companies for many years and both were very experienced and skilled – Dad as a sheet metal worker and Trevor as a welder. In July and August that year they began working evenings and weekends whilst still carrying out their day job at a company they would soon be competing with, Smallwood Bell Ltd in Grove Street, Redditch. Within a couple of months ASGO (The first two letters from Dad's and Trevor's surnames – clever eh!) had picked up enough work for Dad to be able to leave Smallwood Bell and work full time with the company although, it must be said, that most of the money coming in was having to be spent on equipment and overheads.

I remember one afternoon in what was probably the autumn of that year. Dad and Trevor had bought a manual metal guillotine which had to be taken into their first factory at the bottom of Bates Hill. Two problems emerged; firstly, the machine would have to be manually lifted and pushed up approximately 25 concrete steps then along the outside of the building, then into the building and located. Secondly, the machine weighed 2 tons. Me and Peter left school and went to help. Physically, I don't think we have ever worked as hard either before or after but, several hours later and filthy from head to toe, we eventually got the machine into place. That was a job to remember!

Dad bought a very old Imperial typewriter so that Mum (and me sometimes) could type out quotes, invoices, statements and letters. Mum was still working at Boots the Chemist during the early days of ASGO but, within a few years, the accountants told Dad and Trevor that it would make sense tax-wise for Mum and Trevor's wife to become co-directors. Who would have thought, 15 years earlier, that Mum and Dad would be directors of their own company!

I never realised, until I read Dad's book, how scarce money was during the first two years of the business. He recalls at the end of 1968 "*...we went home for Christmas with just £13 each in our pockets... although the three lads never realised, I am afraid that it was a very frugal Christmas for both Jean and I and I have never forgotten that on Boxing Day I hadn't even got the price of a pint in my pocket...*"

Early in 1969, the owners of Smallwood Bell discovered that Dad and Trevor now had their own business and so Trevor was summarily dismissed. ASGO now had to find two full time wages. They also had to buy an old van in order to deliver finished products to customers. The first van they bought was an old Bedford CA model which they hand-painted in battleship grey

The type of Bedford CA van that was used by ASGO.

before getting the company logo painted on the sides. They worked very long hours, starting early and rarely getting home before 9 or 10 o'clock but, ever determined, they built the business up into a flourishing and well-respected company. Eventually, this allowed Mum and Dad to buy their own house in Evesham and for the company to finance company cars for Dad and Trevor. Of course, this meant that Dad was forced to take driving lessons to get his driver's licence.

ASGO went through several moves of location, all in Redditch, before, in 1986 at the age of 65, Dad retired. Just prior to this, several large companies had gone bankrupt whilst owing ASGO significant money running into many thousands. Although the company battled through this crisis it never fully recovered.

Dad later told me that he felt a huge weight lift from his shoulders on the day he left. He walked away without any regrets, a pension in his pocket and the rest of his life to enjoy.

Once Dad had departed, coupled with Trevor's failing health, the company itself began to fail with the added problem that the UK, in the second half of the 1980s, fell into recession. This was the beginning of the end for ASGO and, eventually, the company was dissolved.

I mentioned earlier that Dad was disappointed that none of his sons followed him into the business. To be honest, I am not convinced that one or more of us doing that would necessarily have altered the final outcome. The failing economy of the country sealed the fates of many small and medium sized enterprises. ASGO had been caught up in that net, chewed up and spat out.

That said, what Dad did by forming the company and making so many sacrifices, gave Mum and us a lifestyle we could only have dreamed about years earlier and I am so proud of him for that.

Chapter Thirteen

Radio and Television

IT MIGHT be a strange concept for some readers that, certainly up until the mid-60s, television consisted of just two channels, BBC and ITV. Programmes were broadcast in monochrome, that is, black and white. The picture quality was pretty awful at times and the hours of broadcasting were extremely limited. During the morning all that you could see was what was known as the test card which was supplemented by innocuous music.

The cost of a TV licence in 1963 was £4. This incorporated a licence for a radio too although radio licences were scrapped in the early 1970s. Sometimes there might have been school programmes on during the morning but nothing that you could call entertaining. There were a few programmes on at lunchtime such as *Lunchbox*. This was a low-level entertainment show that lasted about 45 minutes. It was hosted by a very young Noele Gordon who would later find acting fame as motel owner Meg Richardson in the soap opera *Crossroads*. Then there was *Watch with Mother* which, depending upon the day, showed children's programmes such as *The Woodentops, Rag, Tag and Bobtail, Andy Pandy, Tales from the Riverbank* and *The Flowerpot Men*. The television used to close down then until about 5 o'clock when it opened up again and ran until about 11pm – the last programme being a 15-minute religious offering called *The Epilogue*. The very last thing one would see, once the set had been turned off, was the infamous "white dot" on the screen which would then gradually disappear. That was it until the following day! One has to realise firstly that television was not the be all and end all. It was much more important to play with your friends outside. What it did provide, however, was the means to re-enact, when we were playing, what we had seen on shows such as *Dr Who* or *Supercar* (forerunner to programmes such as *Thunderbirds*). Also, if one missed a programme then you simply missed it and had to rely upon friends to tell you what had happened. There was no such thing as video or catch-up. When it was gone it was gone!

In the 1950s and 60s some of the most popular programmes on TV, in our house, were, *Dixon of Dock Green, Hancock's Half Hour, The Black and White Minstrel Show* (in the days long before political correctness), *The Lone Ranger* with Tonto and horse Silver, *Emergency Ward 10, Blue Peter* with the original presenters Christopher Trace, Valerie Singleton and a very young John Noakes with the first Blue Peter dog, Petra and *Thank Your Lucky Stars* with the late, legendary Brian Matthew.

Some of my other favourites included the Gerry and Sylvia Anderson series, *Twizzle, Torchy the Battery Boy, Four Feather Falls, Supercar, Fireball XL5, Stingray and Thunderbirds.*

I'm sure that readers will have their own favourites in addition to these.

In 1967 a series called *The Prisoner* began which was to become something of a cult. This was supposed to be about a former British Intelligence agent who resigned from the Service, but his people wanted to know why and went to all sorts of ridiculous levels to try and find out. Patrick McGoohan starred as "No 6" but, to be honest, viewers really had no idea what was going on. It was futuristic, surreal and wholly unbelievable but riveting at the same time. It ran to just 17 episodes but is constantly re-run all over the world today. The programme was set in The Village – no-one knew where this was meant to be although, in reality, it was filmed at Portmeirion in North Wales, a village designed and built by Sir Clough Williams-Ellis between 1925 and 1975 in the style of an Italian village. Every episode was centred around attempts by No 6 to escape, all of which failed until the last episode which was completely non-understandable and incomprehensible with odd characters appearing in central London, one of which spent the whole episode singing "*Them bones, them bones, them dry bones.*" Such a strange show but one that at school the following day we would thoroughly dissect and analyse.

We used to listen to the radio a great deal. In the early days we had only one. It was a valve-driven radio contained in its own wooden cabinet and which you had to plug into the mains. The radio lived in the kitchen. Once switched on it would take maybe five minutes to warm up before you could hear anything.

There were only three main programmes for the UK. The most widely listened-to service, the *Light Programme*, delivered popular music of the time as well as mainstream light entertainment in the form of variety shows, comedy, and drama. The *Home Service*, whilst it also had its share of general entertainment programmes, was the main channel for news, features, and drama of a more demanding kind – and was also the home of regional programming. The *Third Programme* meanwhile was unashamedly highbrow in character, broadcasting in the evenings only, its output consisting of classical music concerts and recitals, talks on matters scientific, philosophical, and cultural, together with poetry readings and classic or experimental plays. It would be the equivalent of Radio 3 today.

As a child, I remember the radio would always be on while Mum was preparing Sunday lunch. Programmes like *The Billy Cotton Band Show* with Cotton's famous call "Wakey, WAAAAA....KEY!", comedies *The Navy Lark* and *The Clitheroe Kid* with Jimmy Clitheroe were all there but one of the most listened to was *Family Favourites* when listeners would write in and request special music for their loved ones, especially those servicemen stationed abroad. I used to think it was slightly odd that all of these servicemen lived at somewhere called "BFPO." It was a little later in life before I discovered that this meant British Forces Post Office and that the number which followed it identified the country or base at which they were stationed.

Between 5pm and 6pm on Sunday evening we would always listen to *Pick of the Pops* with Alan "Fluff" Freeman – yet another unforgettable theme tune! This was a reverse order run-down of the week's Top Twenty records, especially those that had climbed in the charts. In the summer months during the mid-1960s we would often listen to this whilst sitting on the garden wall of brother and sister Pat and Pam Sabin, great friends who lived around the corner in Pine Tree Close. I can remember being taken, one warm Sunday evening, by the Sabins to watch the speedway at Cradley Heath, about 45 minutes' drive away.

Pat had a transistor radio which we would have quite loud. This would invariably invoke the wrath of Mr. Apperley, a particularly grumpy man who lived next door to the Sabins. He would often come out and shout at us, moaning about the radio and the world in general. We used to call him "old man Apperley"!

By way of contrast, after *Pick of the Pops* came *Sing Something Simple* featuring Cliff Adams and The Cliff Adams Singers with their distinct low-brow, middle-of-the-road renditions of songs which had been popular ten or twenty years previously. Mum and Dad used to like the programme, but it wasn't for me, not at my age then anyway.

On Saturday mornings there was a programme called *Children's Favourites*. This was full of songs and tunes that were popular with young children from *Sparky's Magic Piano, The Boy who Cried Wolf* and *Puff the Magic Dragon* in the late 50s and early 60s to the Mersey sound and beat groups such as The Beatles, The Searchers and The Rolling Stones from 1962.

I can remember when I was 11 or 12, I would be lying in bed on a Sunday night. Martin, by then, had a habit of having a bath quite late on Sundays so that he was prepared for work the next morning (he worked in the drawing office at Alkaline Batteries). He would always have the Top Twenty programme on Radio Luxembourg. I would be treated to all of the hits once more although, as many readers will testify, the Luxembourg signal was notorious for "dropping off station." I wonder how many readers also remember Horace Batchelor. He was an English gambling advertiser, a forerunner I suppose of Bet 365 and the like today. He advertised ways of winning money by predicting the results of football matches. His spelling out of his company address became legendary: "that's Keynsham, K – E – Y – N – S – H – A – M, Keynsham, Bristol."

The Swinging Sixties brought about profound changes in the BBC.

Firstly, in 1964, a programme such as we had never seen on TV made its debut. This was *Top of the Pops*. The first show was broadcast on 1st January 1964 and was presented by the late, and now disgraced, DJ Jimmy Savile. Other original presenters included Alan Freeman, David Jacobs and Pete Murray. Researching the first programme, I can tell you that the running order for the songs played (or more often, mimed) was:

I Wanna Be Your Man	The Rolling Stones
I Only Want To Be With You	Dusty Springfield
Glad All Over	The Dave Clark Five

Stay	The Hollies
Hippy Hippy Shake	The Swinging Blue Jeans
I Want To Hold Your Hand	The Beatles (that week's No 1)

I remember having difficulty when I was young, in saying "Beatles" – it always seemed to come out as "Beakles!"

The BBC recognised that they were losing millions of radio listeners to the increasing number of pirate Radio Stations such as Radio Caroline which broadcast from a moored ship just outside British Territorial waters and therefore outside of British legal jurisdiction. It also started broadcasting in 1964 with DJ's including Tony Blackburn, Simon Dee, Johnnie Walker and Dave Lee Travis, all of whom would later become famous household names and faces with the BBC.

The BBC's radical transformation which had begun with the advent of *Top of the Pops* on TV in 1964 continued with the launch of Radios 1, 2, 3 and 4 in 1967. The Corporation would never be the same again having ridden itself of many "high-brow" tags with which it had become associated since its inception decades before.

Radio 1, the station that, of course, was widely enjoyed by the country's youth, me included, launched on Saturday 30th September 1967 when the newly-recruited Tony Blackburn presented his breakfast show, the first two songs played being *Flowers in the Rain* by The Move followed by *Massachusetts* by the Bee Gees. Although initially sharing each morning with Radio 2, Radio 1 very quickly became its own entity and, as they say, the rest is history.

And so, the genie had been let out of the bottle. The effects of the music and cultural explosion of the 1960s, through radio, television, fashion and the global changes in personal freedoms in particular were the foundation stones that influenced the next 50 years. That all said, I have Dad to thank for my love of the music from the 1930s and 40s. He loved the Big Band sound and would often play music, on Sunday mornings, from Glenn Miller, Tommy Dorsey and others of the World War II era on our tiny "vanity case" Fidelity record player. Even now, and indeed while I am writing these memoirs, I listen to 1940s music on the internet.

Chapter Fourteen

Significant Events

THE 1950s and 1960s were unique and incredible decades significant by the events that took place world-wide – culturally, militarily, scientific, sports and others. Whilst I could simply reel off events that occurred during these periods, that is not the object of these memoirs. I will, therefore, tell you about those that I genuinely remember.

Sputnik and Telstar

I think that, probably, the first major event that I remember, through watching reports on TV and hearing Mum and Dad talking about it, was the launch into space of the Russian communication satellite, Sputnik, in 1957 and the American Telstar satellite 5 years later. I recall more about Telstar as this provided the first live trans-Atlantic television broadcast between Great Britain and America. I watched this live TV link at home on 11th July 1962 in a special edition of *Tomorrow's World* presented at that time by Raymond Baxter. I remember being amazed by these very grainy, scratchy and altogether not very clear pictures that appeared, fully live, from America. I could not even begin to imagine how technology would evolve and develop into what we have today.

Assassination of President John F Kennedy

One of the most vivid events I remember is the reporting of the assassination of President John F Kennedy in Dallas in 1963. The news broke on UK TV around 7pm on 22nd November 1963. Although at the time it didn't mean a great deal to me – I was not quite 10 years old – I remember Mum and Dad being so shocked. I had never seen a grown man cry before so it was shocking for me to see CBS presenter Walter Cronkite with tears in his eyes, announcing the death of the President to the American public. The global mourning that followed very much reminds me of the feelings I experienced some 34 years later when Princess Diana was killed in Paris.

Death of Marilyn Monroe

A few months before the assassination of JFK and, if media reports are to be believed, inextricably linked to him, actress Marilyn Monroe was found dead in her bed, apparently as a result of a drugs overdose. The newspapers, and even at that age I used to read the *Daily Mirror* that Dad would have delivered every morning, were full of conspiracy theories about her death. Rumours had, for a long time, been circulating of romantic links between Monroe and both JFK and his brother, then US Attorney General, Bobby. The theories surrounded the notion that Monroe was out of control and likely to reveal all about her affairs with the brothers. State execution made to look like suicide was a widely held belief at the time, and to some extent, still is to this day. Even Wikipedia, today, describes her death as a "possible suicide."

England World Cup Victory

30th July 1966 is a day that is permanently etched into the minds of every sports fan alive at the time. England won the Jules Rimet Trophy, the football World Cup, beating West German 4-2 in a game that extended into extra-time.

Alf Ramsey, later knighted, had spoken on television in 1963 when he took on the England manager role and said, quite categorically, that in 1966 "We will win the World Cup". This was an astonishing thing to say, and Ramsey was almost ridiculed in some quarters but 3 years later after winning its group stage then defeating Argentina and Portugal in the knock-out stages, England found itself back at Wembley to play out the final against West Germany. Ramsey had found himself the subject of deep controversy following the defeat of Argentina by England, 1-0, in the quarter-final when he referred to the South American team as "animals" because of their violent approach to the game. That was, however, forgotten as the mighty clash with West Germany approached. Only 21 years had elapsed since the end of World War II and so many people, particularly older people, rightly or wrongly, linked the two occasions. Some newspapers were seen to headline phrases such as "We beat them in the War, and we will beat them now." I was glued to the TV (still in black and white, of course) throughout that day and even more so as the 3 o'clock kick off closed in.

The result, England winning 4-2 after extra time, is now a matter of history with Geoff Hurst scoring a hat-trick. But just as historic and heroic was that unforgettable moment when the match was within seconds of finishing and England were leading 3-2. We have all heard it a million times since, but I heard it, live, at the time. The Swiss referee Gottfried Dienst had the whistle to his lips and BBC commentator Kenneth Wolstenholme almost shouted, *"Some people are on the pitch – they think it's all over,"* a split-second later Geoff Hurst scored the fourth England goal, then – *"It is now!"*

I was so happy and so proud that I just burst into tears. It really was one of those moments that one never forgets.

Our World

Our World was the first live, international, satellite television production, which was broadcast, in colour (although we didn't have colour television until the early 1970s) on 25 June 1967. Creative artists, including the Beatles, opera singer Maria Callas, and painter Pablo Picasso – representing nineteen nations – were invited to perform or appear in separate live segments featuring their respective countries. It lasted for over two hours. The Beatles performed *All You Need Is Love* live with many other rock stars and the whole live audience joining in the chorus at the end. Satellite TV had indeed arrived.

Man on The Moon

Another unforgettable time was watching, again on live TV, the Apollo 11 Moon landing on July 20th 1969 followed by the first men to walk on the Moon's surface. From somewhere, Mum and Dad had managed to get hold of an old black and white television which I had in my bedroom and for which I used an old wire coat-hanger as an aerial. The picture was surprisingly good. I had watched the lunar module landing on the lunar surface via a live global satellite link-up. It landed during early evening (although it was only much later that it was revealed there was only 30 seconds worth of fuel left in the craft when it touched down!). I had to wait several more hours, the early hours of the morning in England before the senior astronaut, Neil Armstrong, emerged from the module and started to walk down the ladder. It was a spine-tingling moment of history as he took the final step onto the surface and said those iconic words *"That's one small step for man – one giant leap for mankind."* An automatic camera, attached to one of the legs of the module, captured the moment. Buzz Aldrin was the other astronaut to emerge from the lunar module and walk on the surface. For me, this was awesome, this was the stuff of comic books, this was man landing on another planet – OK, not exactly a planet, but you know what I mean. Armstrong and Aldrin spent 22 hours on the moon, either walking on the surface itself or inside the module. The big question now, however, was – would the lunar module be able to take off as planned? Although many rockets had been tested to get to the Moon, this would be the first ever attempt at a take-off from the Moon. As the scheduled take-off time approached everything was very tense. This really was a leap into the unknown. As the countdown reached zero there were huge sighs of relief in Mission Control, Houston – and at 115 Foxlydiate Crescent – as the take-off was smoothly executed and the module made its way back to the mother craft which had been orbiting the Moon, and manned by the third crew member, Michael Collins. Collins is often described as the unluckiest of men, having flown in several Apollo missions and travelled all the way to the Moon's orbit, but never destined to land there.

As an anecdote, there is a pub on the Redditch Road which sits just inside the Birmingham boundary at Kings Heath. Up until the moon landing it was called the Man *In* The Moon. It changed its name that day to the Man *On* The Moon.

Concorde

Another event sticks in my mind, one that occurred on 2nd March 1969. Supersonic passenger flight had been a dream of aircraft designers for many years. This day was to herald the culmination and combination of dreams and engineering. This was the inaugural flight of Concorde, a British (BAC) and French (Aerospatiale) joint venture project – an aeroplane that could travel at over twice the speed of sound, reducing the flight time between London and New York from over eight hours to a mere three and a half. This first test flight, broadcast live on television (which, of course I watched) lasted for 27 minutes with the aircraft taking off from Toulouse in France. The maiden flight was described as "faultless." I was fortunate enough, years later, to have the opportunity of boarding Concorde at Heathrow Airport – not to fly but just to have a look. It was surprisingly narrow, only two seats on either side of the fuselage, but luxuriously fitted out.

There are many other events that I could tell you about such as the assassinations of Bobby Kennedy and Dr Martin Luther King Jnr, the Vietnam war, the Apollo 13 crisis early in 1970, the first-ever heart transplant by Dr Christian Barnard, Woodstock Music Festival, the Cuban Missile Crisis – the list goes on. These were exceptional years, full of invention, surprise, tragedy and wonder and I am so incredibly lucky to have lived during this time.

Chapter Fifteen

Where it Finishes!

ONCE I decided that it would not be possible, for the reasons I mentioned at the beginning of this book, to go into a great deal of detail about my later working life then this book kind of came to a natural conclusion. But this was never intended to be about later life. Maybe in another book – possibly a fictional account of factual events – at another time that could change. What I wanted to portray to my family, my children, and their children, was what it was like for me growing up in a small town in the 1950s and 1960s. I think that I have achieved that. I have also surprised myself with the things that I recall, mostly with a good deal of fondness but also with some sadness tucked inside as well.

Reading through the pages I realise that I was lucky enough to grow up through incredibly unique times. Britain needed to repair, rebuild and re-invent itself after World War II. Through the 50s and 60s it did just that; culturally, scientifically, politically, industrially, through house-building programmes, music, fashion, and sport. These were two astonishing and remarkable decades. Was that continued through the following decades? Possibly not. When one looks at the years between 1970 and 2000, particularly regarding the decline of manufacturing in the United Kingdom, the huge rises, rightly or wrongly, in immigration into the country, the demise of car and ship building together with the coal and steel industries, the rise in violent crime and demonstrations, financial constraints placed on the National Health Service, the blue light services and the armed forces, I cannot, in all honesty, take the view that Great Britain did itself many favours in the final third of the 20th century.

Did entry to, originally, the Common Market and then the European Union help at all. I think the fact that Great Britain has now parted company with EU, speaks volumes. Will things improve for the future? I have to believe that they will. I also believe, though, that the biggest problems for this planet for future generations will be over-population, climate deterioration and a lack of natural resources, especially water. Our children, their children and future generations need to be smart and brave enough to tackle these problems and to work together with other nations to overcome these problems and to eradicate those things that lead to conflict. That will be long after I am departed from this world, but the challenges are there for all to see.

I apologise if I have made any glaring errors, have got anything horribly wrong or, indeed, if I have forgotten to include anything but this is how I remember it. Enjoy!

Tony Aston
April 2022